The *Ultimate* Teach Your Child to Read Activity Book

DEVELOPING READER

Autumn McKay

The Ultimate Teach Your Child to Read Activity Book: Developing Reader
by Autumn McKay
Published by Creative Ideas Publishing

www.BestMomIdeas.com

Images from Freepik.com

For permissions contact:
Permissions@BestMomIdeas.com

ISBN: 978-1-952016-52-3

The Ultimate Teach Your Child to Read Activity Book: Developing Reader Autumn McKay

My name is Autumn. I am a wife to an incredible husband, and a mother to two precious boys and a sweet little girl!

I have a Bachelor's of Science degree in Early Childhood Education. I have taught in the classroom and as an online teacher. I have earned teacher certifications in Arizona, Colorado, California, and Georgia. However, one of my greatest joys is being a mom! After my first son was born, I wanted to be involved in helping him learn and grow so I began to develop color lessons to help engage his developing mind. I also wanted to help other parents dealing with hectic schedules and continuous time restraints. These activities evolved into my first book, called *Toddler Lesson Plans: Learning Colors*. In the years that followed I continued to develop other books to assist parents who wanted to be involved in teaching their children. (I have also developed a website called BestMomIdeas.com. It's a place where moms are encouraged to be the best version of themselves by feeling understood and never judged.) Through my learning time with my children, I created the following books:

The Ultimate 1 Year Old Activity Book

Toddler Lesson Plans: Learning ABC's

The Ultimate Toddler Activity Guide

The Ultimate Preschool Activity Guide

The Ultimate Kindergarten Prep Guide

Learning Numbers Workbook

Learning Preschool Math Workbook

Learning Kindergarten Math Workbook

Learning 1st Grade Math Workbook

Learning ABC's Workbook: Print

Learning ABC's Workbook: Precursive

Reading is an amazing ability to possess. As my children grew older, I especially wanted to be involved in the unique joy of teaching my children to read. Furthermore, this is a joy I wanted other parents to be able to experience.

Consequently, after teaching my children to read I developed books that would help equip other parents to be involved in the thrill of teaching their children to read. The book you hold in your hands, is one book of a three-book series, to help enable you to accomplish this awesome task of teaching your child to read.

Please Note: The pronoun "he" is often used throughout the text for ease of writing. However, as I wrote each word I was thinking of each little boy AND girl that would do these activities. When feminine pronouns are not used, please do not interpret that as an insult to girls. Girls are awesome!

THE LEARNING TO READ JOURNEY

Welcome to *The Ultimate Teach Your Child to Read Activity Book: Developing Reader* and the exciting journey of teaching your child to read! The majority of those who are reading these words have completed *The Ultimate Teach Your Child to Read Activity Book: Prereading and Beginning Reader* with your child. Wow! I am so proud of you and what you have accomplished in working with your child. I believe you will find *The Ultimate Teach Your Child to Read Activity Book: Developing Reader* to be another great tool for you in helping your child become an accomplished reader.

With the book you hold in your hands, *The Ultimate Teach Your Child to Read Activity Book: Developing Reader*, you will continue in helping your child exercise and develop his knowledge of letters and sounds, and further develop your child's ability in blending the sounds of letters into words. However, the primary focus of the "*Developing Reader*" book is to familiarize your child with diagraphs (two letters that make one sound). This can be difficult for some readers, but as you and your child work through the activities in these pages your child will have taken another significant step in becoming an accomplished reader.

Before moving forward let's look at a synopsis of the *Teach Your Child to Read* series, acknowledging what you have accomplished, as well as commenting on what is in store for you in the following pages.

A BRIEF OVERVIEW OF THE LEARNING TO READ SERIES

Book 1: *The Ultimate Teach Your Child to Read Activity Book: Prereading*

The Ultimate Teach Your Child to Read Activity Book: Prereading focused on phonemic awareness and equipping your child with the necessary skills to learn to read. It is very important for your child to have a strong foundation in phonemic awareness as your child embarks on the journey of becoming an accomplished reader. The "*Prereading*" book helped your child build a solid foundation. The goal in the "*Prereading*" book was to master hearing the sounds (phonemic awareness) before seeing written words. Your child learned to identify upper and lowercase letters, rhyme words, count syllables, blend sounds, and isolate sounds in a word—all of which are fundamental in developing the ability to read.

Book 2: *The Ultimate Teach Your Child to Read Activity Book: Beginning Reader*

As you continued your journey in *The Ultimate Teach Your Child to Read Activity Book: Beginning Reader*, you and your child worked through many lessons to learn how to decode words. Your child learned how to use his finger to point to letters in the word, say the sound, and slide his finger under the word to blend it together. This is an important skill that he will continue to use in *The Ultimate Teach Your Child to Read Activity Book: Developing Reader* (Book 3). Eventually your child began to read sentences and even short stories, and now he is ready to move forward to learn the complex reading sounds.

Book 3: *The Ultimate Teach Your Child to Read Activity Book: Developing Reader*

You are currently holding *The Ultimate Teach Your Child to Read Activity Book: Developing Reader* in your hands. You will now introduce your child to complex reading sounds—digraphs—through fun lessons and stories.

Digraphs are two letters that make one sound. The sounds represented by digraphs are often different from the sounds normally represented by the individual letters that make up the digraph. For example, "ar" makes the sound /ar/ (said "R"), like in the word "MARK" rather than /m/ /a/ /r/ /k/. Digraphs can be made up of two consonants (Ex. "ch"), two vowels (Ex. "oo"), a consonant and a vowel (Ex. "ew"), or two vowels separated by a consonant (Ex. "a_e").

Digraphs can be tricky for new and young readers, so please take your time as you go through each lesson. It's important that your child continues to stay confident in his abilities as a reader (and love reading), so don't hesitate to repeat activities within a lesson if you feel your child is not ready to move forward.

The "*Developing Reader*" book is presented in lessons, just like the "*Beginning Reader*" book. Each lesson will include *Flashcards*, a few fun activities to practice the new digraph sound, and a story for your child to practice reading. It is recommended to print *Flashcards* on cardstock for sturdiness and durability throughout all of the lessons.

When your child learns a new digraph sound, there are an abundance of new words for your child to learn for that particular sound. So, as an added bonus I have included *Bonus Flashcards* that include all words associated with the new sound in the printable appendix. Please follow this link to access the *Bonus Flashcards*:

Your child will continue to feel proud as he reads short stories in the "*Developing Reader*" book. This is an accomplishment that should be celebrated, so cheer him on as he continues to learn, grow, and read! Exposure to short sentences and stories using words he is familiar with, will help build his confidence and fluency (read like he talks) as a reader.

After your child has learned all the digraphs, he will continue to enhance his reading fluency through fun activities. Reading fluency is helping your child read in a natural, smooth voice with expression (reading like he talks). Being a fluent reader allows your child to focus less on sounding out words and more on understanding the text. Being a fluent reader allows your child to concentrate on comprehending the text he is reading.

A REVIEW OF IMPORTANT TOPICS

In the introduction of *The Ultimate Teach Your Child to Read Activity Book: Prereading and Beginning Reader* I addressed several significant topics. Topics included: The Importance of Reading, The Value of the Printed Page, Read to Your Child, Signs of Reading Readiness, Repetition Required, Paying Attention to Font and Practice Makes Progress. There would be value in reading these topics if you are new to this series. There is also value in rereading each of those topics if you need a refresher. It is important for you to review **Read to Your Child, Repetition Required, Paying Attention to Font, and Practice Makes Progress** whether you are new or continuing your learning to read journey because of its direct impact on your child's ability to read. This information will hopefully help you as you strive to be the best teacher for your child.

READ TO YOUR CHILD

There are numerous benefits to reading with your child. Reading helps develop important language skills. Exposure to a wide variety of language from fairy tales, science books, comic books, and history books helps develop a child's vocabulary in a way that everyday conversation cannot. Language in a book is typically more grammatically correct than spoken language, and language in books offers more diverse or rare vocabulary than spoken language—even in children's books.

Reading to our children allows them to experience places they might otherwise not be able to visit. Reading allows our children to learn about different cultures, experience the history of different places, and explore the beautiful sights of the world. All of these literary "world travels" might inspire your child to travel the world one day or become a lifelong learner of other cultures.

Reading helps engage and expand the mind. It can encourage our children to think creatively and use their imagination whether in play, creating their own stories, or in school. Reading is like exercise for the brain. It helps keep the brain engaged and at tip top shape. Reading allows us to be exposed to more ideas and different forms of thinking, nurturing intellect and understanding.

How can your child be exposed to all of the benefits of reading if he can't read? It can happen because of you. He can still receive the benefits of reading if you read to him. Throughout this entire reading journey, and even after he is a fluent reader, please continue to read to your child. Reading together helps build comprehension skills when you discuss what was read, cultivates a love of reading, and most importantly—creates a special bond between you and your child.

Here are a few tips to remember as you read to your child:

1. **Point to the words of the story as you read.** This will help your child develop print awareness; he will begin to understand that words are read from left to right and top to bottom.

2. **Sound out random words in the story.** For your child to be successful in learning to read he will need to master the "blending" technique (I will discuss this in more detail in a few pages), so it will be helpful for him to hear you sound out words in a story. To do this, pick a word on the page, break the word apart into phonemes (sounds), and then blend the sounds together to say the complete word.

If you would like to view a demonstration, please visit this link:

www.bestmomideas.com/developing-reader-videos

3. **As you read together, ask questions about the text.** This will help build reading comprehension and communication skills. Reading comprehension is not a skill we will focus on mastering until your child has become a fluent reader, but it's a good skill to practice when reading together.

REPETITION REQUIRED

As a parent, I often need to repeat directives to my children to put their shoes on, clean up their toys, or not throw balls in the house. Frequently, the statement to "not throw balls in the house" needs to be repeated because it doesn't quite "stick" the first time. After my children have heard "do not throw balls in the house," multiple times on different occasions, they will (hopefully) rethink releasing the ball as they wind up.

Repetition is essential in helping a child learn. Your child needs to hear an idea more than one time for it to "stick" in his brain. When your child attends school, many learning concepts will be reviewed and retaught at each grade level. This is to help your child truly learn, understand, be able to recall, and apply the concepts taught.

Throughout this "*Teach Your Child to Read*" Series I have taken the same approach that "repetition is important." Key concepts or skills (like rhyming or blending) will be taught and practiced over and over again. Occasionally, there will be one activity repeated for learning two different word sets. This learning method is beneficial in helping the concept "stick" as your child learns to read. I want to make sure your child masters the skills needed to make this a smooth journey for you and your child.

PAYING ATTENTION TO FONT

It may seem strange that I am addressing the use of fonts in a book which is purposed to help a child read. However, sometimes issues that seem insignificant can have a significant impact. As much as possible it is wise to eliminate any potential issue that may hinder your child's growth in his or her reading ability.

Children's books and various texts use a variety of different fonts. Some of these fonts have a silly "a" and others have a silly "g." With some fonts the uppercase "I" looks like a lowercase "l". Similarly, some fonts might have too many curls making it distracting for a child to concentrate on the words of the text. This can be very confusing for a child learning to read.

When teaching your child to read, it's best to use a consistent font throughout the process—a font that resembles the style of handwriting you will also teach your child, that is evenly spaced between letters, and has simple letters. For this reason, I have chosen to use *Comic Sans MS* for all materials where your child will practice reading skills. *Comic Sans MS* has a "normal" looking "a" and "g." It has a distinction between a lowercase "l" and uppercase "I," and has nice spacing between letters making it easier for your child to read the text. If you choose to print materials for your child, please consider using the *Comic Sans MS* font, as well.

The progress your child makes during this journey is dependent on you and your child. To make this journey successful, it is best to be consistent with daily practice (even if the weekends consist only of you reading to your child). Remember, the more often a child sees or hears the same information the more likely it will "stick" in his brain.

With that said, I am not going to make a claim that your child will be able to read in "X" number of weeks. Every child learns differently and at a different pace. Move at a pace that is comfortable for you and your child. You know your child best, therefore you are the best person to determine the correct pace your child should learn. If you see your child is struggling, then slow down, evaluate what he is struggling with, and reteach any activities or lessons that would help him gain the knowledge he needs to move forward without frustrations.

There is absolutely no shame if it takes one child longer to learn to read than another child. The time it takes a child to learn to read does not determine his future success with reading. Reading success is determined by having a strong foundation in phonics and continuous practice of reading.

THE LEARNING TO READ PROCESS

The following information is foundational material that is repeated in each of the *Teach Your Child to Read Books*. Please do not move ahead to the activities prior to reviewing this material. It would also be wise to periodically read through these pages, to help you as you strive to become an accomplished reading teacher.

As you prepare to teach your child, I want you to be equipped and prepared in such a manner that you feel overly qualified and confident to assist your child in his or her learning to read journey. The reality is, whether intentional or not, as you interact with your child you WILL BE (whether at a traffic stop sign or at the grocery store) teaching your child to read. Unfortunately, some parents do a poor job. Thus, I want you to be well equipped and the best version of a "reading teacher" that you can possibly be.

In the following pages are important terms and teaching methods with which you need to become familiar. Alright, maybe you don't need to know them, and you could move ahead to the activity pages and begin...but let's do this right. Remember, there are few investments in your child's life that are more important than nurturing your child's ability to read. If your child becomes an accomplished reader, it will significantly enhance his or her ability to succeed in the "challenges of life." An "accomplished reader" needs an "accomplished teacher" and you are the best person in your child's life to fill that role.

TERMINOLOGY

Term	Definition	Example
Analytic Phonics	A teaching of reading through word association and identifying similarities between words	m + at c + at f + at
Blending	Combining individual phonemes (sounds) into a whole word	s-n-a-p -> snap
Consonant	All letters that are not a vowel	b, c, d, f, g, h, j...
CVC Words	Consonant + vowel + consonant word	d o g C V C
Digraph	A group of two letters with a single sound	Bean - "ea" says /ē/
Fluency	The ability to read words in a limited time interval —freedom from word decoding	
Grapheme	A letter or group of letters representing one sound	sh, ch, th
Long Vowel Sound	Where the sound of the vowel is the name of the vowel	The letter "a" in "day" makes the sound /ā/
Phoneme	Basic sound of a letter	"b" says "buh"
Phonemic Awareness	The knowledge that words are made of individual sounds	The word "map" has 3 sounds. /m/ /a/ /p/
Short Vowel Sound	The sound that most often corresponds with vowels	The letter "e" in "net" makes the sound /ě/

Sight Word	An irregular word that does not follow phonetic rules and must be memorized	the, to, me
Syllable	A unit of sound made up of a vowel sound or a vowel consonant combination	watermelon wa-ter-mel-on
Synthetic Phonics	Teaching reading where each phoneme (sound) is pronounced in isolation	fish /f/ /i/ /sh/
Vowel	a, e, i, o, u, and sometimes y	

THE SOUNDS OF THE AMAZING ALPHABET

There are 26 letters in the alphabet, but there are over 44 phonemes (sounds) represented by the letters or combination of letters. In addition, many of the 44+ phonemes have multiple ways of representing the same sound. For instance, the phoneme /ai/ (said "A") can have the following representations: /ā/ in "MAPLE," /ay/ in "SAY," /a_e/ in "MATE," or /ea/ in "BREAK." It is also important to recognize that one grapheme (combination of letters) can have multiple pronunciations. For example, the grapheme "ea" from the word "BREAK" also makes the /ee/ sound in the words "SEA, SPEAK, TEAM."

PHONEME (letter sound) CHART

Consonants:

Phoneme (sound)	**Grapheme** (letter or group of letters that represent the sound)	**Examples**
/b/	b, bb	big, rubber
/d/	d, dd, ed	dog, add, filled
/f/	f, ph	fish, phone

Phoneme (sound)	Grapheme (letter or group of letters that represent the sound)	Examples
/g/	g, gg	go, egg
/h/	h	hot
/j/	j, g, ge, dge	jet, cage, barge, judge
/k/	c, k, ch, ch, cc, que	cat, kitten, duck, school, occur, antique
/l/	l, ll	leg, bell
/m/	m, mm, mb	mad, hammer, lamb
/n/	n, nn, kn, gn	no, dinner, knee, gnome
/p/	p, pp	pie, apple
/r/	r, rr, wr	run, marry, write
/s/	s, se, ss, c, ce, sc	sun, mouse, dress, city, ice, science
/t/	t, tt, ed	top, letter, stopped
/v/	v, ve	vet, give
/w/	w	wet
/y/	y, i	yes, onion
/z/	z, zz, ze, s, se, x	zip, fizz, sneeze, laser, is, please, xylophone

Consonant Digraphs:

Phoneme (sound)	Grapheme (letter or group of letters that represent the sound)	Examples
/th/ (not voiced)	th	thumb
/th/ (voiced)	th	this
/ng/	ng, n	sing, monkey
/sh/	sh, ss, ch, ti, ci	ship, mission, chef, motion, special
/ch/	ch, tch	chip, match
/zh/	ge, s	garage, measure
/wh/	wh	what

Short Vowel Sounds:

Phoneme (sound)	Grapheme (letter or group of letters that represent the sound)	Examples
/ă/	a, au	hat, laugh
/ĕ/	e, ea	bed, bread
/ĭ/	i	if
/ŏ/	o, a, au, aw, ough	hot, want, haul, draw, bought
/ŭ/	u, o	up, ton

Long Vowel Sounds:

Phoneme (sound)	Grapheme (letter or group of letters that represent the sound)	Examples
/ā/	a, a_e, ay, ai, ey, ei	bacon, late, day, train, they, eight
/ē/	e, e_e, ea, ee, ey, ie, y	me, these, beat, feet, key, chief, baby
/ī/	i, i_e, igh, y, ie	find, ride, light, fly, pie
/ō/	o, o_e, oa, ou, ow	no, note, boat, soul, row
/ū/	u, u_e, ew	human, use, few

Other Vowel Sounds:

Phoneme (sound)	Grapheme (letter or group of letters that represent the sound)	Examples
/oo/	oo, u, oul	book, put, could
/ōō/	oo, u, u_e	moon, truth, rule
/ow/	ow, ou, ou_e	cow, out, mouse
/oy/	oi, oy	coin, toy

Strong R Sounds:

Phoneme (sound)	Grapheme (letter or group of letters that represent the sound)	Examples
/ar/	ar	car
/ār/	air, ear, are	chair, bear, care
/ir/	irr, ere, eer	mirror, here, cheer
/or/	or, ore, oor	for, core, door
/ur/	ur, ir, er, ear, or, ar	burn, first, fern, heard, work, dollar

SIGHT WORDS

When I was earning my degree to become a teacher, many reading programs made children memorize "sight words" to help children learn to read. You might be familiar with Dolch word lists—those are considered high frequency words that are used very often in readings—they are sometimes referred to as sight words too. However, I don't believe this is a beneficial way to teach a child to learn to read. Let me explain. Learning to read through sight words teaches a child to memorize words. Often with a new reader, he is not going to memorize the word based on the letters that make up the word, but by the shape of the word. For instance, "IN, ON, and AN" all have the same shape configuration—all the same letter heights and length of letters in the words. If a child was memorizing the words and trying to recall one of the sight words he memorized then he might mistake "ON" for "AN" or even "IN."

Many of the sight words on a Dolch word list can be phonetically sounded out; therefore, there is no need to memorize these words. When a child comes across these "sight words," he can decode the word by simply using the same method of reading he has used throughout the whole learning to read process of sounding it out and blending the word together.

However, there are a few words that do not follow the rules of phonics, like the words "THE" and "YOUR." Those words, and others that do not follow phonetic rules, will be treated as "sight words" that your child will memorize instead of sounding out. Your child will probably try to sound out the "sight words" at first because that is what he has been taught to do, but just remind him that the "sight words" are words that don't follow the rules and have to be memorized, so his brain will have to remember how the word looks.

I will introduce the rule breaker "sight words" in various activities, so please concentrate on teaching your child to read phonetically unless it is clearly stated to teach a word as a "sight word."

MANY SOUNDS, DON'T BE DISCOURAGED

All of these rules, loopholes, and exception to rules, can make teaching your child to read seem impossible, but I am here to tell you it is possible. I will be with you as you brave this journey! We will start simple so your child can build a strong foundation of reading knowledge and confidence. This will help make reading fun and enjoyable.

PHONEMIC AWARENESS, SYNTHETIC PHONICS, AND ANALYTIC PHONICS

Being a former schoolteacher and having taught my three children to read, I have had the most success in teaching children to read using phonemic awareness, synthetic phonics, and a little bit of analytic phonics. (You may recall reading definitions of these terms earlier, but I will explain them in more detail in the preceding paragraphs). Since I have had success using this process in the classroom and with my own children, I am confident this process will be successful in helping you teach your child to read. Here is a more detailed explanation of phonemic awareness, synthetic phonics, and analytic phonics.

Phonemic Awareness – This is the ability to hear, identify and manipulate phonemes (sounds). For example, the word "CAT" has three phonemes (sounds) that make up the word -- /k/, /a/, and /t/. Phonemic awareness also involves the ability to change the /k/ sound in "CAT" to /m/ to make a new word, "MAT."

When you see the slashes (/) around a letter that indicates the letter sound, not the letter name.

Synthetic Phonics – This is the process of identifying the phonemes (sounds) letters of a word into and then combining (blending) the sounds to form a word. For example, if a child sees the word "RUN," he would identify the letters, say the sounds for the letters /r/, /u/, and /n/, and then blend the sounds together to form the word "RUN."

Analytic Phonics – This is when a child is able to look at a whole word and use his knowledge of similar words to decode the word. You might have heard someone refer to this type of phonics as a "word family." For example, if your child came across the word "FAT," for the first time, and has read the words, "CAT, MAT, SAT, and BAT" before, then he might be able to break the word "FAT" apart into known sounds or parts and use his knowledge to decode (pronounce) the new word that is similar to words he knows.

Phonemic awareness and synthetic phonics are the most important processes in learning to read. In the simplest terms, phonemic awareness is about helping a child identify the sounds of a word and synthetic phonics helps a child learn how to blend the sounds to form a word. Analytic phonics (word families) is easier for some children and harder for others; that is why I use it sparingly. Don't stress if your child doesn't understand analytic phonics (word families). He will still be able to read successfully as long as he can identify sounds (phonemic awareness) and blend (synthetic phonics).

FOCUSING ON SYNTHETIC PHONICS AND BLENDING

With synthetic phonics your child is learning how to blend sounds together to form words. Blending means that your child is able to say the individual phonemes (sounds) of a word and connect the sounds together smoothly to say a word. Blending is a super important skill that your child will need when learning to read. When your child is able to blend, he can decode words quickly and more effectively. With practice, your child will become skilled at blending and recognizing familiar words and will no longer need to sound out every word. However, in the beginning stages of reading it is very important to practice blending words.

CHOPPY AND SMOOTH BLENDING

There are two types of blending—choppy and smooth.

Choppy Blending – This is when you make the individual sounds of a word. For example, the word "SAT" would be /s/ /a/ /t/.

Smooth Blending – This is when you stretch out the sounds of the word so they seem like they are connected. For example, using the same word, "SAT," you would stretch out the sounds to be "ssssaaat."

If you would like to view a demonstration, please visit this link:

www.bestmomideas.com/developing-reader-videos

Choppy blending allows a child to hear the individual sounds of a word, but when you have a new reader, it might take your child a few seconds to recall an individual sound in the word. Therefore, as he is sounding out the word "SAT," he might know that "S" says /s/, then pause to think that "A" says /a/, and pause once more to think that "T" says /t/. By the time he finishes sounding out the word it could take five to six seconds and he might have forgotten what the first sound was that he made. Choppy blending makes it a little more difficult for new readers to connect the first sound to the last sound. This type of blending might be more frustrating for younger or newer readers.

I prefer to use smooth blending when teaching children to read. By stretching out the sounds, it helps the sounds stay connected to each other, to more easily put the word together after it is sounded out. However, you will notice in the example above of "SAT" that some letters cannot be stretched out (T). The letters or sounds would sound distorted if you tried to stretch them out. In this case, you simply make the short individual sound of the letter or sound, "ssssaaaat." Sounds that cannot be stretched include—/b/, /d/, /g/, /k/, /p/, /t/, /ch/.

In this book there will be some activities for you and your child to do together to help practice the blending technique orally. When your child is able to blend orally, it makes it easier to blend printed words. So, please, please practice the blending activities in this book. Once you have practiced them, practice them again and again. This will help make your child's learning to read journey a success.

(As your child's teacher, you will need to be able to demonstrate the proper phonemes (sounds) and blending techniques to your child. Knowing the correct pronunciation of phonemes will help your child to be more successful on his reading journey. If you need to familiarize yourself with any phonemes or blending techniques use this link to access the demonstration videos:......)

www.bestmomideas.com/developing-reader-videos

Learning to read is a huge milestone for any learner. There will likely be some hurdles to overcome. I will list a few below and some strategies to help get your reader get back on track. However, you know your child best. If you feel that your child might be struggling beyond these hurdles and have a learning disability, I recommend jotting down your concerns—write specific instances that lead you to believe your child is in need of help. Share these concerns with your child's doctor and teacher. Don't be scared to be an advocate for your child!

1. **Your child is just not ready.** Children develop at different rates and ages. Just because one child is reading at age five doesn't mean every child will be ready to read at age five.

2. **You are not reading TO your child enough.** Your child might learn all the foundations for reading, but seem to be struggling to read fluently. He needs to hear an example of a fluent reader, so it is best if you continue to read to your child throughout this entire journey.

3. **Physical impairment.** Maybe your child is having difficulty reading because the letters he sees are blurry. He might need glasses. Perhaps your child is not understanding the sounds each letter makes because his hearing is impaired. These are situations that have a solution, so please check with your doctor.

4. **Your child needs more background information.** Sometimes children that have trouble comprehending a text don't have enough knowledge of the world to understand the reading. For example, if a child is reading a baseball story, but has never seen a baseball field, talked about the player's positions, or listened to other baseball stories, then he will have a difficult time grasping what is going on in the story.

5. **Your child is flipping letters or letter sounds.** Reading is new to your child. It's very common for new readers to flip letters (especially "d" and "b") and their sounds. It will take time and continuous practice for your child to correct this mistake. Calmly, correct his or her mistake.

(Numbers 5 and 6 are common reading hurdles, but they could also be signs of dyslexia. Dyslexia is an assortment of reading issues relating to decoding words and comprehension skills. If you believe your child might be dyslexic it is best to get it addressed as a young reader. Nevertheless, being dyslexic is in no way a hinderance to your child's future learning potential.)

7. **Your child is afraid to fail.** Sometimes children are anxious to try new things because they fear failure. Talk to your child to understand his or her anxiety. Make sure you are providing a safe environment for your child to make mistakes and learn from mistakes. Be supportive and encouraging.

8. **Your child does not enjoy reading.** This could simply be a matter of your need to become more selective with the books you provide your child. Take time to really think about your child's interests, and provide books accordingly. Many boys find nonfiction (real-life) books more enjoyable. My little girl loves reading about animals and princesses.

YOU CAN DO IT!

As a teacher, I am so appreciative of parents who invest their lives in their children. I am encouraged that you care about your child's education and want to see your child become a fluent reader. I believe in you. I believe whether your child is a beginning reader, reader in progress, or a struggling reader, you will be able to teach him or her to read with success.

I am also excited for you as you begin this journey. Yes, there will be frustrating moments but please remember that you are your child's best advocate and teacher. In purchasing this book, you have already demonstrated your care and concern for your child. You will succeed and it is my desire to assist you in this endeavor.

As noted, my goal with this series is to provide you with a step-by-step guide to help teach you how to teach your child to read. I will be your coach, mentor, and guide throughout this journey. But rest assured, if you cannot find the answer or help you need in these books you can reach me by email or phone with any questions:

Autumn@BestMomIdeas.com

678.400.9032

Finally, I want to reinforce what you and I both know...the task is secondary to your relationship with your child. One of the most important parts of this learning process is the time you spend with your child. Relish the moments you sit and read with your child. Embrace watching your child grow and learn. Take pleasure in witnessing his or her confidence grow in leaps and bounds. Go at a pace that is suitable for you and your child, and find joy in your day, as you learn to read together!

Activity Time >

As you begin Activity Time in this book, please remember the importance of how you manage this time with your child. Following the preceding suggestions will help you (and your child) gain the most benefit from your activity time together with your child.

TOOLS FOR A SUCCESSFUL LEARNING TIME

As you begin these learning activities, here are a few suggestions I found extremely helpful in creating the most productive "activity and learning times" with my children. Granted, you know your child best, but in most cases I believe you will find the following ideas beneficial.

1. **Create a Routine** – Things tend to flow better when routines are in place. Establishing a learning routine, helps a child have a learning mindset. He knows what is expected of him during the learning time. The routine does not have to be a strict time schedule; it can be simply based on the structure of the day. For example, after breakfast is learning to read time, but breakfast could be at 8:30am one morning and 9am the next day. Your child would still understand that after breakfast it is time to prepare for reading.

2. **Praise Hard Work** – Praising your child's efforts and work ethic helps motivate him to continue working hard. If your child is receiving positive feedback about trying hard, even if he made a mistake, he will be willing to try hard again. Whereas, praising your child's "smarts" might prevent him from accepting new challenges due to fear of failing and losing the title of "smart."

3. **Take Breaks** – Learning to read is a journey. For some children it is a long, hard journey (although, my hope is that these activities make it easier), for other children the journey is quick. Truly, even the best child can have a rough day. A speedy learner can struggle. The sweetest child can become frustrated. This journey will require a lot of patience—patience from you and patience from your child. There will be frustrations for you and/or your child during the learning process. When it happens, stop the activity, take a break, and come back when you are both ready. Do your best to keep reading a positive experience so that your child continues to enjoy reading!

4. **Turn Things into a Game** – If one lesson or activity seems too boring for your child, try turning it into a game or a friendly competition. It's always fun (and a great confidence booster) to defeat mom or dad in a reading competition.

5. **Point to Letters to Sound Out, Swipe Finger Under Word** – It is important for a beginning reader to point to the letters of a word as he is sounding out a word because it helps the brain connect the sounds and word together. This will help the formation of the word begin to "stick" in his brain as he continues to see the same word.

Children often follow the example of their parents. If you are not pointing at words when you are reading to your child, there is the possibility your child will do likewise. If this is the case, set an example for him and begin using your finger to read. You can also explain how using his finger is like a magic reading tool that helps his brain remember words.

6. **Cover Words to Help Concentration** – Often times a new reader can become overwhelmed with the amount of text or illustrations on a page of a book. Even though he has a strong foundation in reading, due to the volume of words on a page he is distracted or unable to concentrate on what he is reading. If you notice this, allow him time to look at the illustration on the page (this can help provide clues for the text he will be reading) and then use a plain piece of white paper or Guided Reading Strips to cover the page of the book— cover all, but one line. This will help your child be able to focus.

See video demonstration at **www.bestmomideas.com/developing-reader-videos**.

7. **Be a Great Example! - The example you set in life for your child is very important. When it comes to Activity Time, it is critical that you are pronouncing the sounds of the various letters correctly.** Your pronunciation of letters and words will be emulated by your child. Let me stress this point again: It is extremely important that your pronunciations are correct. Before you begin each lesson, please familiarize yourself with the correct pronunciation of the letter sound your child will be introduced to in the lesson. This can be found in the previous section (page xviii) entitled "*Learning to Read Process.*" You can also visit this link to find a video clip containing the proper pronunciations needed for each lesson:

www.bestmomideas.com/developing-reader-videos

8. **Resources:**

a. **Create a Salt Tray** – This is an resource that will be used throughout *The Ultimate Teach Your Child to Read Activity Books: Beginning Reader* and *Developing Reader*. A salt tray allows your child to connect the formation of the letter and letter sound in their brain. You will need a cookie sheet with edges and salt.

b. **Foam, Magnetic or Wooden Letters** – It is important to have tactile letters on hand for many of the activities. Please purchase uppercase and lowercase foam or wooden letters. If you can't find a combination of both uppercase and lowercase, then please purchase lowercase letters.

To access the printable, full-color Appendix, *Flashcards*, *Bonus Flashcards* and *Stories* please visit this link:

www.bestmomideas.com/developing-reader-appendix

Password: **bestmomideas2px7**

To access the video demonstrations please visit this link:

www.bestmomideas.com/developing-reader-videos

Lessons

To access the printable, full-color Appendix, *Flashcards*, *Bonus Flashcards*, and *Stories* please visit this link:

www.bestmomideas.com/developing-reader-appendix

Password: **bestmomideas2px7**

Activity 1

MATERIALS:

- ☐ *Vowel House* Activity Pages (Appendix A)
- ☐ Crayons
- ☐ Scissors
- ☐ Glue

DIRECTIONS:

1. There are five *Vowel House* activity pages you need for this activity. You can choose to do this activity in a single day or multiple days.

2. In this activity you will teach your child there are five vowels in the alphabet, "a, e, i, o, u" and that every word has at least one vowel in the word. Tell your child that any letter that is not a vowel is called a consonant.

3. Place the "Aa" *Vowel House* activity page in front of your child.

4. Explain to him that he will color the pictures on the right-hand side of the page.

5. He will read the word under the picture. Instruct him that each of these words has the vowel "a" in it. The "a" in these words makes a short "a" sound of /ă/ (said "ah").

6. Ask him to cut out each picture and glue it into the "Aa" house.

7. Repeat Steps 3-6 with the E, I, O, and U *Vowel House* activity pages.

Activity 2

MATERIALS:

- ☐ *Vowel Flowers* Activity Page (Appendix B)
- ☐ Crayons

DIRECTIONS:

1. 1. Place the Vowel Flowers activity page in front of your child.

2. Explain to your child that each of these words on the activity is a short vowel sound. Go over the short vowels sounds with your child. /ă/, /ĕ/, /ĭ/, /ŏ/, /ŭ/

3. Ask him to read the word inside each flower.

4. Next, instruct him to color the flower based on the color code key. Words with the vowel "a" will be colored blue. Words with the vowel "e" will be colored orange. Words with the vowel "I" will be colored yellow. Words with the vowel "o" will be colored red. Words with the vowel "u" will be colored green.

cut along line

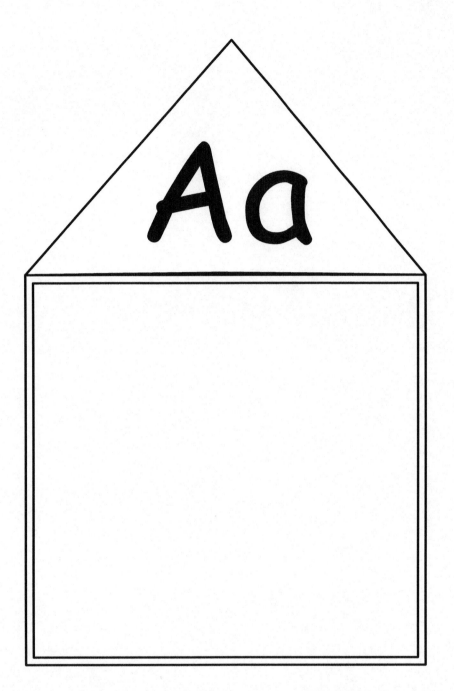

hat

map

jam

stamp

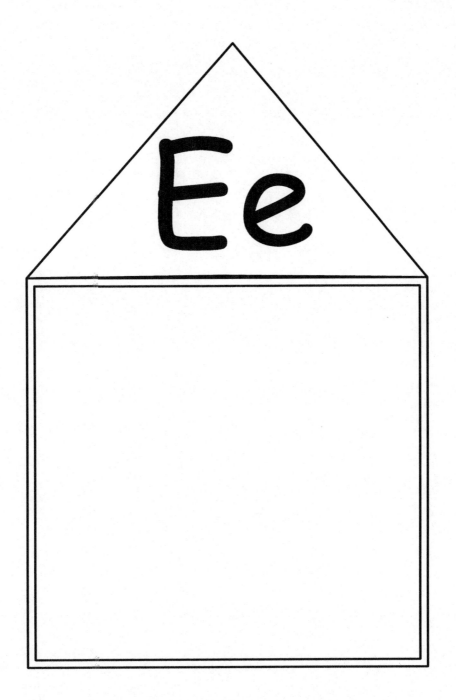

Ee

jet

web

bell

10
ten

cut along line

Ii

pig

lips

mitt

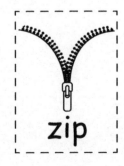

zip

Lesson 1

cut along line

Oo

lock

mop

frog

pot

Lesson 1

cut along line

bus

cup

sun

duck

Lesson 1

cut along line

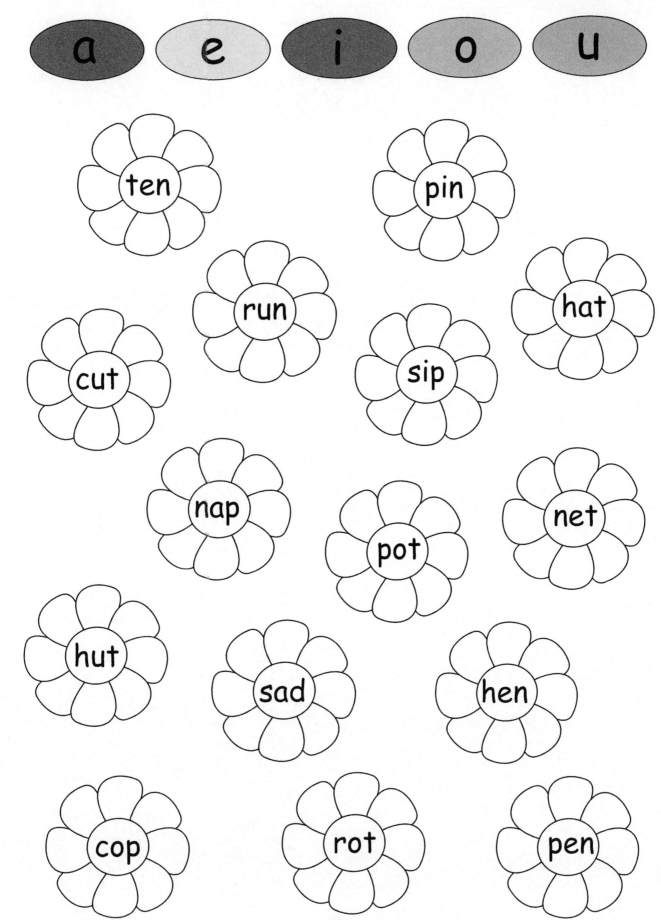

a e i o u

ten

pin

run

hat

cut

sip

nap

pot

net

hut

sad

hen

cop

rot

pen

Lesson 1

{ **New Words: shed, dish, fish, bash, cash, dash, mash, flash, rash, crash, ship, shop,** }

Bonus Flashcards included in printable appendix:
shot, shack, shrub, finish, shut, wish
Visit bestmomideas.com/developing-reader-appendix
Password: bestmomideas2px7

Activity 1

MATERIALS:

- ☐ *Sh Maze* Activity Page (Appendix C)
- ☐ Pencil

DIRECTIONS:

1. Tell your child that he will learn a new sound today. The sound is /sh/, said "ssshh." Tell him that this sound is made up of two letters, "s" and "h." When the "s" and "h" are beside each other they make the sound /sh/.

2. Provide him with some examples of words that have the sound /sh/. For example, fish, cash, trash, ship, shark, shirt.

3. Place the *Sh Maze* activity page in front of your child.

4. Tell him that he will begin at "Start" and use his pencil to follow the /sh/ sound through the maze. The /sh/ sound will be at the beginning or end of the word.

   Answer Key: Start > shirt > shell > shovel > fish > trash > cash > shoe > sheep > Finish

Lesson 2

Activity 2

MATERIALS:

- ☐ *Flashcards* for Lesson 2
- ☐ Playdough

DIRECTIONS:

1. In this activity your child will practice reading the *Flashcards* for Lesson 2. As he reads each *Flashcard* ask him to locate the vowel in the word.

2. After your child locates the vowel in the word, instruct your child to form a small "u" shape with playdough to place over the vowel. This is called a breve. It helps the reader know that the vowel is a short vowel sound.

3. Ask your child to tell you the short vowel sound located in the word on the *Flashcard*.

4. For example, with the word "shed," your child will place his finger under the letters to sound out each sound of the word and then slide his finger under the word to blend the sounds together to form the word. After he has read the word, he will locate the vowel—"e." Next, he will place a breve made of playdough over the "e" in the word "shed." Lastly, he will tell you the short "e" sound--/ĕ/.

Activity 3

MATERIALS:

- ☐ *Sh Sentences* Activity Page (Appendix D)
- ☐ Pencil

DIRECTIONS:

1. Present the *Sh Sentences* activity page to your child.

2. Ask your child to read the words in the Answer Key box.

3. Instruct your child to read a sentence from the activity page and select the word from the Answer Key that completes the sentence.

4. Ask your child to write the word in the blank.

5. Repeat Steps 3 and 4 until all sentences are complete.

   Answer Key:

   1. Fish   2. Shed

   3. Shrub   4. Ship

   5. Finish

Stories

Locate the Lesson 2 story titled "Todd's Trip" on the next page. Fold the story into a book. Ask your child to read the story to you as many times as he would enjoy.

Optional comprehension questions to ask your child:

1. Where do you think Todd went on his trip?

2. What kind of things did Todd see?

3. What did Todd buy?

Lesson 2

shed

dish

fish

bash

cash

dash

mash

flash

rash

crash

ship

shop

cut along line

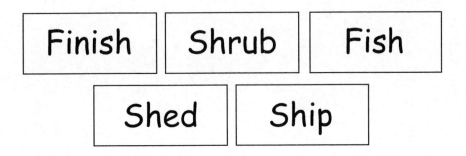

Finish	Shrub	Fish
Shed	Ship	

1- The _____ swims under the dock.

2- Dad went in the _____.

3- Mom trims the _____.

4- The _____ gets stuck in the sand.

5- She will _____ the run.

cut along line

3

Todd went into a shop. He picks up a shell. Todd hands cash to the man to get the shell.

2

Todd is on a trip. Todd spots a ship.

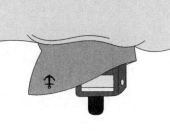

Todd steps on a dock. He spots a red fish flash past 4 him.

Todd's Trip

Lesson 2

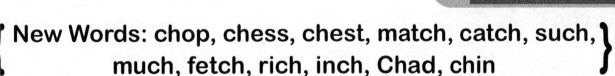

{ **New Words: chop, chess, chest, match, catch, such,** **much, fetch, rich, inch, Chad, chin** }

Bonus Flashcards included in printable appendix:

itch, check, pitch, patch, punch, chill, hatch, witch, munch, latch,

chimp, champ, chick, batch, lunch, branch, switch, crunch

Activity 1

DIRECTIONS:

1. Explain to your child that he will learn a new sound today. The sound is /ch/, said "ch" like a choo choo train. Tell him that this sound is made up of two letters, "c" and "h." When the "c" and "h" are beside each other they make the sound /ch/.

2. Ask your child to pretend to be an alligator who snacks on /ch/ sounds. (He will hopefully love the idea!)

3. Explain to your child that you will "call out" several words. Some of the words will have the /ch/ sound and some will not. Tell your child that he can use his arms to "chomp like an alligator" when he hears the /ch/ sound in a word.

4. Here is a list of words:

   chop, wish, monkey, crunch, banana, hatch, sit, chin, switch, light, check

Lesson 3

Activity 2

MATERIALS:

- ☐ *Chimp Finger Puppet* Activity Page (Appendix E)
- ☐ *Flashcards* for Lesson 3
- ☐ Crayons
- ☐ Scissors
- ☐ Glue, Stapler, or Tape

DIRECTIONS:

1. Present your child with the *Chimp Finger Puppet* activity page.

2. Instruct him to color the chimp.

3. When he has finished coloring, cut out the front and back sides of the chimp.

4. If needed, assist your child in assembling the chimp puppet by placing the front side of the chimp on top of the backside of the chimp. Glue, staple, or tape around the edges of the chimp puppet.

5. Allow your child to try on his new finger puppet.

6. Explain to him he made a chimp and the word "chimp" starts with the sound /ch/. His chimp is going to help him read his new words.

7. Place a *Flashcard* for Lesson 3 in front of your child. Allow him to use his chimp to point to the letters of the word and say the sound of the letter(s). Ask him to slide the chimp across the bottom of the word as he sounds out the word.

8. Complete Step 7 for all of Lesson 3 *Flashcards*. Take breaks as needed.

Activity 3

MATERIALS:

☐ *Flashcards*
☐ 5 Post-It Notes
☐ Marker

DIRECTIONS:

1. Tell your child that in this activity he will practice hearing and reading short vowel sounds. On the five Post-It Notes write a lowercase vowel (ă, ĕ, ĭ, ŏ, ŭ) with a breve (the little u) over the letter. One letter is written on each Post-It Note.

2. Place the Post-It Notes on the table or floor six inches apart.

3. Gather the *Flashcards* for Lesson 2 and 3.

4. Explain to your child that he will sound out and read the word on the *Flashcard*. Then he will determine which short vowel sound he hears in the word.

5. Next, he will place the *Flashcard* on top of the corresponding short vowel Post-It Note.

6. Continue until all *Flashcards* are sorted taking breaks when necessary.

• • •

Stories

Locate the Lesson 3 story titled "Pumpkin Patch." Fold the story into a book. Ask your child to read the story to you as many times as he would enjoy.

Optional comprehension questions to ask your child:

1. Where does Chad go?

2. What does Chad see at the pumpkin patch?

3. Have you ever been to a pumpkin patch?

The Ultimate Teach Your Child to Read Activity Book: Developing Reader **Autumn McKay**

chop

chess

chest

match

catch

such

much

fetch

rich

inch

Chad

chin

cut along line

Lesson 3

3

Chad spots a witch at the pumpkin patch. He trips on a big pumpkin.

2

Chad had lunch. Next, he went to the pumpkin patch.

Chad gets the big pumpkin. He had so much fun!

4

Pumpkin Patch

Lesson 3

1

cut along line

{ New Words: where, want }

Activity 1

MATERIALS:

☐ *Small, Medium, Large* Activity Page (Appendix F)
☐ Markers
☐ *Flashcards* for Lesson 4

DIRECTIONS:

1. Tell your child that (as in Book 2: the "*Beginning Reader*"), he will be introduced to sight words. Sight words do not follow the rules for sounding out a word. (In assisting your child, you will pronounce the word for him and ask your child to repeat the word.)

2. Show your child the *Flashcard* "where." Point to the word, say the word, and ask him to repeat the word back to you.

3. Repeat Step 2 with the *Flashcard* for "want."

4. Use the *Flashcards* for Lesson 4. In addition, select 10 sight words *Flashcards* your child has learned from *The Ultimate Teach Your Child to Read Activity Book: Beginning Reader* (the, here, to, my, a, what, be, of, you, so, come, put, I, there, was, he, she, do, your, all, give, have).

5. Show your child the *Small, Medium, Large* activity page.

6. Ask your child to choose a *Flashcard* and read the sight word on the *Flashcard*. Then he will write the sight word in small letters.

7. Ask your child to read the sight word again, and write the sight word in medium letters.

8. Finally, instruct you child to read the sight word and write the word in large letters.

9. Complete Steps 6-8 until all sight words are written.

Stories

Locate the Lesson 4 story titled "The Fish." Fold the story into a book. Ask your child to read the story to you as many times as he would enjoy.

Optional comprehension questions to ask your child:

1. What is the person trying to find?

2. In what type of home do you think the fish lives (ocean, lake, river, fish tank)?

3. Where did he find the fish?

where

want

small **medium** large

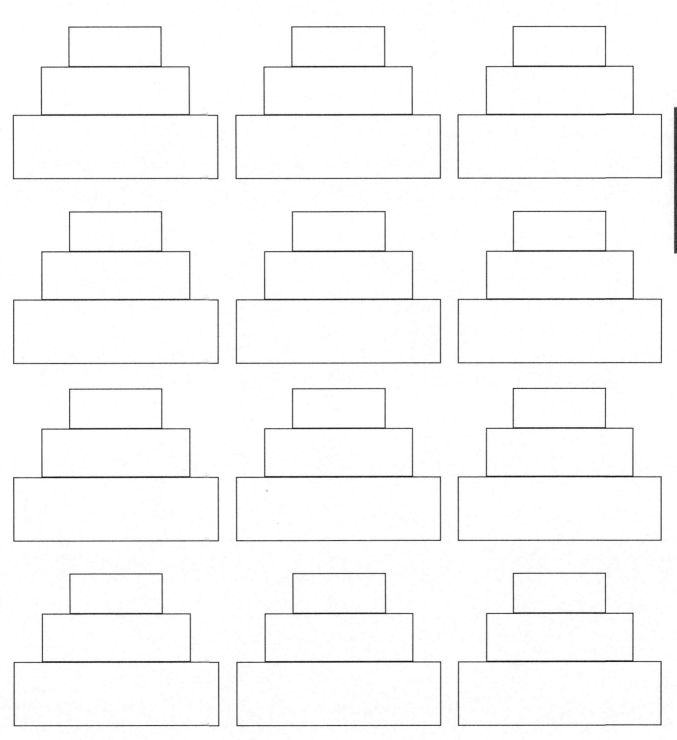

Lesson 4

3

I will check next to the
sunken ship. I have a
hunch he is there.

2

Where is the fish? I can't
spot the fish.

The Fish

I spot the fish past the
ship. He is next to the
chest.

Lesson 4

1

{ **New Words: that, this, then, than, bath, math, path, with, sixth, thin, thick, them** }

Bonus Flashcards included in printable appendix:

cloth, thrill, bathtub

Activity 1

MATERIALS:
☐ *Th Puzzle* Activity Pages (Appendix G)
☐ Scissors
☐ Glue

DIRECTIONS:
1. Tell your child that he will learn a new sound today. The sound is /th/, said "thh." Explain to him that this sound is made up of two letters, "t" and "h." When the "t" and "h" are beside each other they make the sound /th/.

2. Cut out each puzzle piece on the second page of the *Th Puzzle* activity page.

3. Hand your child the first activity page of the *Th Puzzle*. Ask him what sound the "th" says.

4. Hand your child the puzzle pieces. Explain that each picture starts with the /th/ sound.

5. Ask him to identify the pictures one at a time and glue them in their correct locations on the *Th Puzzle* (first page).

   Answer Key for Pictures: three, thief, throw, thumb, thorn, throat, thick, think, thunder, thermos, thigh, thousand, thimble

6. Complete the puzzle.

Activity 2

MATERIALS:

☐ *Th Mapping* Activity Page (Appendix H)
☐ Crayons

DIRECTIONS:

1. Tell to your child that he will be mapping out words today.

2. Show him the mapping chart on the *Th Mapping* activity page. Explain that he will use the chart to map the words listed under the chart.

3. Go over the chart with your child. Tell your child that when he finds a short vowel sound in a word, he will place a breve (little u) over the vowel in the word. When he sees a digraph (two letters that make one sound) in the word, he will draw a box around the digraph. For this particular lesson the box will go around the "th" digraph.

   (You can show him the code for long vowel sounds and silent letters; however, he will not learn long vowel sounds until Lesson 13. Long vowel sounds are when the vowel says its name.)

4. Each code is color coded. For this lesson, your child will need a green and purple crayon.

5. Ask him to look at the first word, "that."

6. Ask him if he sees a "th" digraph in the word "that." Ask him to use the purple crayon to draw a box around the "th."

7. Now, ask him to place his finger under the word to sound out the word.

8. Ask your child if he heard a short vowel sound in the word "that." Once he has indicated the short "a" vowel sound, ask him to draw a green breve over the "a."

9. Ask him to read the word again.

10. Continue mapping the remaining 11 words.

    Answer Key:

    1. that-breve over "a," purple box around "th"

    2. this-breve over "i," purple box around "th"

    3. then-breve over "e," purple box around "th"

    4. than-breve over "a," purple box around "th"

    5. bath-breve over "a," purple box around "th"

    6. math-breve over "a," purple box around "th"

    7. path-breve over "a," purple box around "th"

The Ultimate Teach Your Child to Read Activity Book: Developing Reader Autumn McKay

Answer Key:

8. with-breve over "i," purple box around "th"

9. thick-breve over "i," purple box around "th"

10. cloth-breve over "o," purple box around "th"

11. thrill-breve over "i," purple box around "th"

12. sixth-breve over "i," purple box around "th"

• • •

Activity 3

MATERIALS:

☐ *Sound Out and Write* Activity Page (Appendix I)
☐ Pencil

DIRECTIONS:

1. Show your child the *Sound Out and Spell* activity page.

2. Explain to him that he will look at the picture on the left-hand side of the page and identify the picture.

3. Next, he will sound out the word while circling the letters that spell the word.

4. Instruct your child to write the word based on the letters he circled on the lines provided on the right-hand side of the page. If your child is learning letter formation, please write the letters using a yellow marker and ask him to trace the letters you have written.

5. Lastly, he will read the word he wrote to determine if it matches the picture.

    Answer Key:

    1. Path

    2. Shed

    3. Inch

    4. Math

    5. Chick

    6. Ship

    7. Bath

    8. Fish

cut along line

that

this

then

than

bath

math

path

with

sixth

thin

thick

them

cut along line

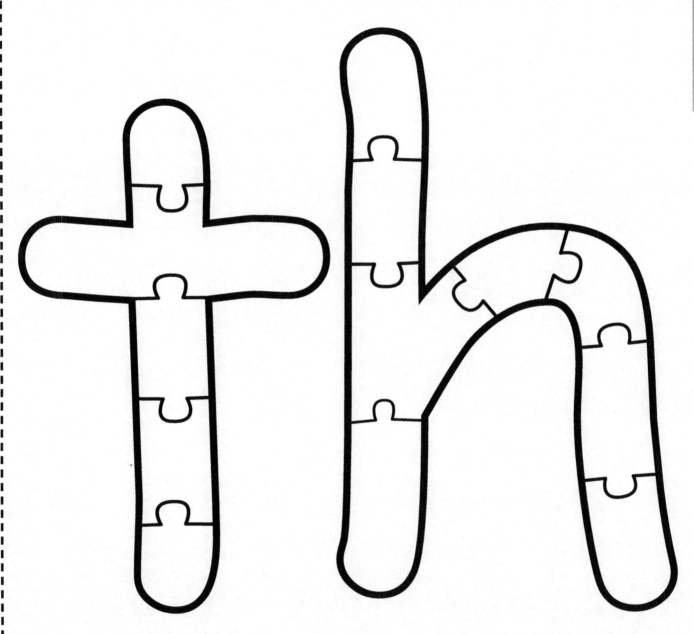

cut along line

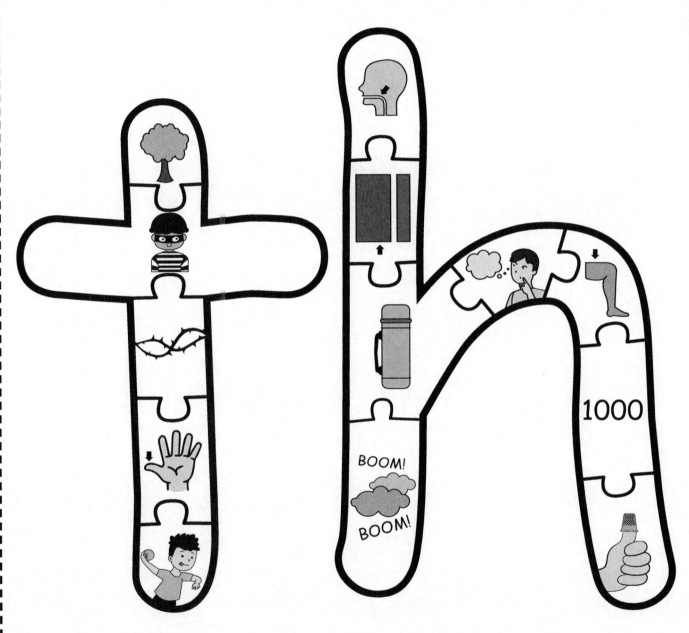

Phonics Skills	Code	Example
short vowel	⌣	căt
long vowel	—	cāke
silent letters	/	bik√
digraphs	▭	t͞hat

cut along line

that   path

this   with

then   thick

than   cloth

bath   thrill

math   sixth

cut along line

	p b	a e	sh th
	sh ch	e i	d p
	a i	n m	th ch
$\begin{array}{r} 2 \\ +2 \\ \hline 4 \end{array}$	h m	a u	th sh
	ch th	o i	ss ck
	th sh	i e	w p
	b r	o a	th ch
	f h	i u	sh th

3

Beth must mix this and that in a dish.

2

Beth wants muffins. She will fix a batch with Mom.

Muffins

Then, Beth will bake the muffins. She and Mom munch on a muffin.

4

Lesson 5

1

{ New Words: when, whip, which, whick, whack, whiff }

Activity 1

MATERIALS:

☐ *Flashcards* for Lesson 6
☐ Wooden or Magnetic Letters

DIRECTIONS:

1. Tell your child that he will learn a new sound today. The sound is /wh/, said "wuh." Explain to him that this sound is made up of two letters, "w" and "h." When the "w" and "h" are beside each other they make the sound /wh/.

2. Use the *Flashcards* from Lesson 6 for this lesson. (New Words: when, whip, which, whisk, whack, whiff)

3. Lay out the wooden letters w, h, e, n, i, p, c, s, k, a, f, f, h in the middle of the table or floor. Explain to your child that you will sound out a word and he will need to find the correct letters and place them in the correct order to read the word.

4. Smoothly sound out the word on the *Flashcard*. For example, the word "when" would be sounded out, "weenn."

5. Ask your child what sound he heard at the beginning of the word and instruct him to find the letters among the group of letters on the table. (It might be helpful to remind your child that the beginning sound of these words will be formed by two letters.)

6. Now ask your child what sound he heard next (feel free to sound the word out again) and instruct him to locate that letter and place it beside the first letters. Continue until the entire word is spelled out.

7. After your child has found the correct letters, ask him to point to the letters to sound them out and slide his finger across the bottom of the word as he reads the word.

8. Place the letters back in the group of letters and repeat Steps 4-7 with the remaining *Flashcards* you selected.

Lesson 6

Activity 2

MATERIALS:

☐ 25 Craft Sticks
☐ Marker
☐ Mason Jar

DIRECTIONS:

1. Choose 20 *Flashcards* from Lessons 1-6.

2. Write these words at the end of each craft stick (one word per craft stick).

3. On the 5 extra craft sticks, write "Oh Snap" (on 2 sticks), "Pick 2," "Take a Stick," and "Read and Keep."

4. Place all craft sticks, word down, into a Mason jar.

5. Ask your child to join you in a game of "Oh Snap!"

6. Explain to your child that you will take turns selecting a craft stick from the Mason jar. You must read the word on the stick. If you read the word correctly, then you get to keep it, if you read it incorrectly you must put it back in the jar. The first player that collects seven sticks wins.

7. However, if a player draws an "Oh Snap" stick then he must put all of his sticks back in the jar and start over.

8. If a player draws a "Pick 2" stick, then he gets to choose two craft sticks from the jar to read and keep.

9. If a player draws a "Take a Stick" stick, then he gets to take a stick from an opponent.

10. If a player draws a "Read and Keep" stick, then the player draws and reads as many sticks in 10 seconds as he can and keeps the sticks read correctly.

11. As you are playing this activity with your child, be sure to sound out words in a smooth or choppy blend so he can hear the blends of the word. (You might even read a few words "wrong" to give him an advantage.)

12. Enjoy playing!

Stories

Locate the Lesson 6 story titled "I Help.". Fold the story into a book. Ask your child to read the story to you as many times as he would enjoy.

Optional comprehension questions to ask your child:

1. Do you think the child likes helping Dad?

2. Do you like to help your parents with chores?

3. On page 4, it says "I lug the stuff back to the shed." What do you think lug means?

Lesson 6

when

whip

which

whisk

whack

whiff

3

Dad trims the shrubs. Whack! I pick up the branch which is thick.

2

Dad cuts the grass. I help him.

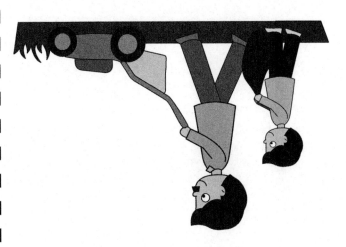

When Dad and I finish, I lug the stuff back to the shed.

4

Lesson 6

I Help

Lesson 6

{ **New Words: are, arm, car, art, cart, card, cards, far, farm, tart, chart, shark** }

Bonus Flashcards included in printable appendix:

part, dart, start, smart, bar, barn, bark, park, mark, market, dark, spark, mart, hard, star, warm, harm, scar, march, sharp, charm, marsh, scarf, swarm, garden, artist

Activity 1

MATERIALS:

☐ *Flashcards* for Lesson 7

DIRECTIONS:

1. Explain to your child that he will learn a new sound today. The sound is /ar/, said "r." Tell him that this sound is made up of two letters, "a" and "r." When the "a" and "r" are beside each other they make the sound /ar/.

2. You and your child you be singing a song today, and to make it more fun I recommend dressing up as pirates or acting like pirates.

3. Sing this song with your child to the tune of "Yo Ho." This song is adapted from Wallace Farms Blog.

The Pirate Sound
There once was a pirate long ago
Who loved the a-r sound you know
When he saw a word with an a and r
You could hear him calling near and far

Car, jar...ar, ar, ar
Art, mart...ar, ar, ar
Dart, part....ar, ar, ar
Arm, harm, charm

That pirate sailed the ocean blue
In search of gold and silver too
But the greatest treasure that there could be
Was an a-r word that he could read

Bar, scar...ar, ar, ar
Tart, chart...ar, ar, ar,
Park, shark...ar, ar, ar
Bark, park, mark

Ar, ar
Ar, ar
Ar, ar
An a-r word says ar, ar

Lesson 7

4. Allow your child to practice reading the *Flashcards* for Lesson 7 to you.

Activity 2

MATERIALS:

☐ *Shark Attack* Activity Pages (Appendix J)
☐ Scissors

DIRECTIONS:

1. Cut out the red and blue sharks on the second *Shark Attack* activity page.

2. Show your child the first *Shark Attack* activity page (the game board).

3. Ask him if he would like to be the red sharks or blue sharks. Hand him the desired shark cut-outs.

4. Explain to your child that the object of the game is to get four of his colored sharks in a row. The sharks can be placed horizontally, vertically, or diagonally.

5. The first player will select a square. The player must read the word in the square correctly to place a colored shark in the square.

6. Then the next player will take a turn by choosing a square, reading the word in the square, and placing his colored shark on the square.

7. Continue playing until one player has four of his colored sharks in a row.

8. The first player to get four sharks in a row wins!

• • •

Stories

Locate the Lesson 7 story titled "At the Farm." Fold the story into a book. Ask your child to read the story to you as many times as he would enjoy.

Optional comprehension questions to ask your child:

1. What does the child do at the farm?

2. What kind of job would you like to do at the farm?

3. Did the child have fun at the farm? Why do you think so?

are

arm

car

art

cart

card

cards

far

farm

tart

chart

shark

shake	arm	are	bar	market	hard	marsh
car	cart	card	barn	spark	star	sharp
tart	chart	start	dark	park	harm	charm
dart	part	smart	mark	mart	scar	garden
far	cards	farm	bark	art	warm	scarf

Pick to use the red sharks or blue sharks as your game pieces. Then choose a word from the board to read. If you read it correctly, place your colored shark on top of the word you read. The next player will then choose a word to read and place a different colored shark on the word read. Your goal is to read 4 words in a row horizontally, diagonally, or vertically. You also must block your opponent from reading 4 words in a row.

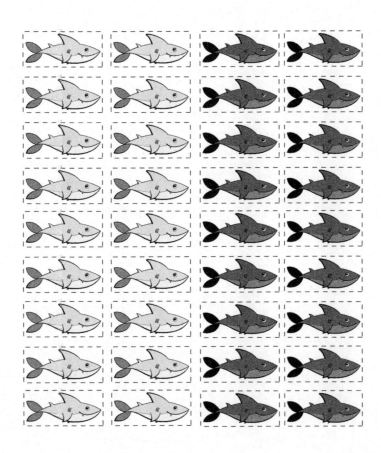

3

The barn is big and red.
The dog barks.

2

At the farm, I fetch the chicks a snack in the garden.

At the Farm

Lesson 7

cut along line

{ New Words: said, too, other }

Activity 1

MATERIALS:

- ☐ *Sight Word Caterpillars* Activity Page (Appendix K)
- ☐ Marker
- ☐ Circle Label Stickers

DIRECTIONS:

1. On the circle label stickers, write the individual letters for the following sight words: said, too, other, where, want, all, give, have, do, your. Each sticker should only have one letter written on it. For example, you will need four stickers for the word "said;" a sticker for "s," "a," "i," and "d."

2. Tell your child that he will learn three new sight words today. Remind your child that sight words do not follow the rules for sounding out a word. After pronouncing each word on the *Flashcards* for Lesson 8, ask your child to repeat the word. Practice the sight words several times.

3. Show your child the *Sight Word Caterpillars* activity page.

4. Ask him to choose a caterpillar on the activity page.

5. Ask him to read the sight word on the caterpillar's body.

6. Now, ask him to find the matching label sticker letters to place on the caterpillar's body.

7. Once all of the stickers for the sight word have been placed on the caterpillar, then your child can read the sight word again.

8. Repeat Steps 4-7 until all caterpillars are complete.

Lesson 8

Stories

Locate the Lesson 8 story titled "To the Market." Fold the story into a book. Ask your child to read the story to you as many times as he would enjoy.

Quotation marks have already been taught in Lesson 25 of The Ultimate Teach Your Child to Read Activity Book: Beginning Reader. However, as noted repetition is important in the learning process. On page 3, please show your child the quotation marks and remind him that when he sees quotation marks it shows that someone is speaking.

Optional comprehension questions to ask your child:

1. Where did Trish go?

2. What is a market?

3. What is Trish looking for?

4. Who does Trish ask for help?

said

too

other

cut along line

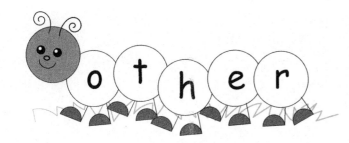

Lesson 8

Lesson 8

To the Market

Lesson 8

1

Trish is off to the market. She will pick a cart when she gets there.

2

It is hard to spot the carrots. The market boss said, "I can help."

3

The boss steps to the carrots. Trish said, "Thanks."

4

cut along line

{**New Words: for, fork, cork, pork, torn, worn, corn, born, work, porch, short, north**}

Bonus Flashcards included in printable appendix:

form, word, worth, worst, sport, storm, actor, color, porch, thorn, factor, doctor, export, inform, forgot

Activity 1

MATERIALS:

- ☐ *Or Book* Activity Pages (Appendix L)
- ☐ Scissors
- ☐ Crayons
- ☐ Stapler

DIRECTIONS:

1. Tell your child that he will learn a new sound today. The sound is /or/, said "oar." Explain to him that this sound is made up of two letters, "o" and "r." When the "o" and "r" are beside each other they make the sound /or/.

2. Show your child the *Or Book* activity pages.

3. Ask him to cut each page in half along the dotted line.

4. Place the book in the following order: title page, find it page, read it page, write it page, picture it page. Staple the pages together.

5. Ask your child to color the title page.

6. Ask him to turn to the "Find It" page. Ask him to color all of the "or" digraphs he can find.

7. Ask him to turn to the "Read It" page. Ask him to place his finger under each letter/digraph to sound out and read the words on the page. (Remember that you can use a piece of paper or guided reading strip to cover words not being read.)

8. Ask your child to turn to the "Write It" page. Ask him to trace the letters of each word, and then sound out and read the word.

9. Ask him to turn to the "Picture It" page. Instruct your child to identify the pictures on the page. Ask him to color the pictures that have the /or/ sound in the word.

   Answer Key: fork, corn, porch, thorn, doctor, torn

Activity 2

MATERIALS:

- ☐ *Flashcards* for Lesson 9
- ☐ Objects Around the House

DIRECTIONS:

1. Cut out the *Flashcards* for Lesson 9: for, fork, cork, pork, torn, worn, corn, born, work, word, form, north, short, worth, worst, sport, storm, actor, color, porch, thorn, factor, doctor, export, inform, forgot.

2. Create an obstacle course in your home for your child. Here are some examples of obstacles to include:

   1. Hop from pillow to pillow.

   2. Crawl under a table.

   3. Climb a mountain of pillows.

   4. Zoom a toy car along a piece of tape.

   5. Walk backwards around an island.

   6. Army crawl under a row of chairs.

3. As you create the obstacle course, place *Flashcards* throughout the course.

4. Explain to your child that he will need to complete the obstacle course, but as he is working his way through the obstacle course, he will find cards with words that he must read before moving forward.

5. Cheer him on as he makes his way through the course.

Activity 3

MATERIALS:

☐ Shaving Cream

DIRECTIONS:

1. Spread shaving cream onto a tabletop or counter.

2. Select 10 *Flashcards* from varying Lessons.

3. Explain to your child that you will slowly sound out a word. He will need to listen very carefully because he will be writing the letters to the sounds he hears to spell the word.

4. Slowly and smoothly sound out the first word.

5. Ask your child what sound he heard first and to write the sound in the shaving cream. Remind him that some sounds are made by two letters beside each other.

6. Ask him what sound he heard second, third, and so forth until he completes the writing of the word.

7. Ask him to read the word he wrote to you.

8. Check to see if it is spelled correctly.

9. He may erase the word and repeat Steps 4-8 with the other nine *Flashcards*.

● ● ●

Stories

Locate the Lesson 9 story titled "The Fort." Fold the story into a book. Ask your child to read the story to you as many times as he would enjoy.

Optional comprehension questions to ask your child:

1. Who builds a fort?

2. Where do they build a fort?

3. What do they use to build a fort?

4. Have you ever built a fort?

for

fork

cork

pork

torn

worn

corn

born

work

porch

short

north

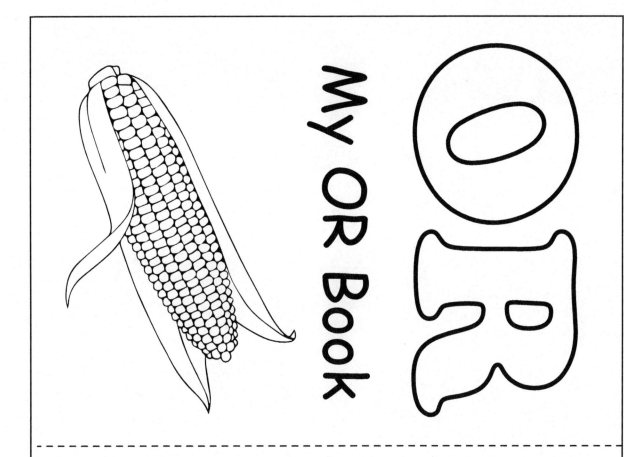

OR

My OR Book

Find it

sh	wo	am	rn
er	ox	fr	ir
mi	ch	he	th
ck	re	bo	ca
lo	wh	ri	ex
ar	hi	yo	or

Read it

for
fork
born
word
form
north
storm

Write it

pork
work
form
north
storm

cut along line

Picture it

cut along line

Lesson 9

Bob and Sam want to form a fort. It will be on the porch.

2

cut along line

3

Bob will form the fort with a thick blanket. Sam will work with a box.

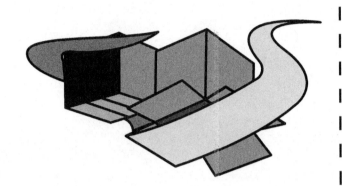

Bob and Sam finish. Sam checks that the fort will not crash. Bob climbs in the fort.

4

The Fort

Lesson 9

1

{ **New Words: her, term, fern, verb, after, sister, girl, bird, third, shirt, churn, surf** }

Bonus Flashcards included in printable appendix:

mother, father, brother, under, never, order, offer, river, clerk, stern, person, better, summer, letter, winter, soccer, sir, firm, dirt, stir, their, first, skirt, chirp, twirl, spirit, thirst, fur, turn, hurt, burn, curb, curl, burst, burger

Activity 1

DIRECTIONS:

1. Tell your child that he will learn a new sound today. The sound is pronounced "errr" (like putting on brakes), but three different groups of letters make this same sound— "er, ir, and ur."

2. Explain to your child that he will be pretending to drive a car. (He may sit and drive his car or he may walk around the room and drive his car.)

3. Tell your child that as he drives his car you will slowly call out a list of words (see step 4). If he hears a word with the /er/, /ir/, or /ur/ sound then he will slam on his brakes in his car and say "errr."

4. Here is a list of words you may call out: germ, king, fork, mother, girl, whale, burn, first, pen, soccer, color, bird

Activity 2

MATERIALS:

☐ *Flashcards* for Lesson 10
☐ 3 Pieces of Paper
☐ Marker

DIRECTIONS:

1. On the first piece of paper write in large, lowercase font "er." On the second piece of paper write in large, lowercase font "ir." And, on the third piece of paper write in large, lowercase font "ur."

2. Lay each piece of paper on the floor six inches from each other.

3. Gather the *Flashcards* for Lesson 10 and shuffle them.

4. Explain to your child that you will hold up a *Flashcard*. He will sound out the word to read it. Then he will place it on the correct piece of paper on the floor for which digraph the word contains—"er, ir, ur."

   For example, the word "letter" would be placed on the "er" piece of paper.

5. Continue playing until all *Flashcards* are read and sorted.

Activity 3

MATERIALS:

☐ *Er, ir, ur Mapping* Activity Page (Appendix M)
☐ Crayons

DIRECTIONS:

1. Explain to your child that he will be mapping out words today.

2. Show him the mapping chart on the *Er, ir, ur Mapping* activity page. Explain that he will use the chart to map the words listed under the chart.

3. Go over the chart with your child. Explain that when he finds a short vowel sound in a word, he will place a breve (little u) over the vowel in the word. When he sees a digraph (two letters that make one sound) in the word, he will draw a box around the digraph—there can be two digraphs in one word.

   You can show him the code for long vowel sounds and silent letters; however, he will not learn long vowel sounds until Lesson 13. (Long vowel sounds are when the vowel says its name.)

4. Each code is color coded. For this lesson, your child will need a green and purple crayon.

5. Ask him to look at the first word, "father."

6. Ask him if he sees a digraph in the word. Ask him to use the purple crayon to draw a box around the "th" and another purple box around "er."

7. Now, ask him to place his finger under the word to sound out the word.

8. Ask your child if he heard a short vowel sound in the word "father." Once he has indicated the short "a" vowel sound, ask him to draw a green breve over the "a."

9. Ask him to read the word again.

10. Continue mapping the remaining seven words.

    Answer Key:

    1. father- breve over "a," purple box around "th" and "er"

    2. summer- breve over "u," purple box around "er"

    3. burger- purple box around "ur" and "er"

    4. shirt- purple box around "sh" and "ir"

    5. verb- purple box around "er"

    6. thirst- purple box around "th" and "ir"

    7. churn- purple box around "ch" and "ur"

    8. their- breve over "e," purple box around "th" and "ir"

Activity 4

MATERIALS:

☐ *Snakes and Ladders* Activity Page (Appendix N)
☐ Dice
☐ 2+ Game Pieces

DIRECTIONS:

1. Show your child the *Snakes and Ladders* activity page.

2. Explain to him that you both will be playing a reading game. Other family members are welcome to play too.

3. Make sure everyone has a game piece. Place all game pieces on start.

4. The youngest player will go first.

5. He will roll the dice and move the respective number of spaces.

6. If a player lands on a ladder space, he may climb the ladder up to the higher space. If he lands on a snake, then he must slide down the snake's back to the lower space.

7. Once he has landed on his space, he will read the word inside the box. If he reads the word incorrectly, he must go backwards one space.

8. Now, the play moves to the next person.

9. Continue playing until a player reaches the end of the game.

● ● ●

Stories

Locate the Lesson 10 story titled "The Skirt.". Fold the story into a book. Ask your child to read the story to you as many times as he would enjoy.

Optional comprehension questions to ask your child:

1. What is the girl wearing?

2. What color is her skirt?

3. What do you do when you receive new clothes?

her

term

fern

verb

after

sister

girl

bird

third

shirt

churn

surf

Phonics Skills	Code	Example
short vowel	⌣	căt
long vowel	—	cāke
silent letters	/	bik/e
digraphs	▭	t̲h̲at

father   verb

summer   thirst

burger   chūrn

shirt   their

cut along line

cut along line

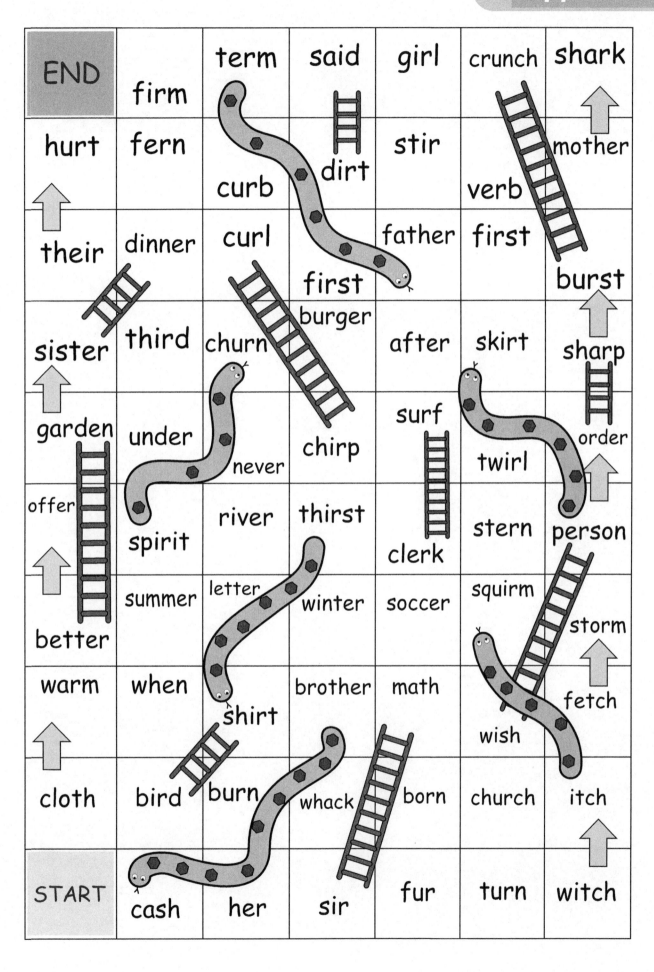

END — firm — term — said — girl — crunch — shark

hurt — fern — dirt — stir — verb — mother

their — dinner — curb — curl — father — first — burst

sister — third — churn — first — burger — after — skirt — sharp — surf — order

garden — under — never — chirp — twirl

offer — spirit — river — thirst — stern — person — squirm — storm — fetch

better — summer — letter — winter — soccer — wish

warm — when — shirt — brother — math

cloth — bird — burn — whack — born — church — itch

START — cash — her — sir — fur — turn — witch

3

The girl twists and turns in her skirt.

2

The girl has on a red skirt. She has never worn a skirt.

The girl is glad when her skirt twirls.

The Skirt

4

Lesson 10

1

cut along line

{**New Words: hung, lung, long, song, strong, bang, hang, king, wing, sing, finger, nothing**}

Bonus Flashcards included in printable appendix:

ring, ding, sang, rang, fang, doing, swung, swing, sting, during, living

Activity 1

MATERIALS:

☐ *Build It, Write It* Activity Page (Appendix O)
☐ Wooden Letters
☐ Pencil

DIRECTIONS:

1. Tell your child that he will learn a new sound today. The sound is /ng/, said "eng." Explain to him that this sound is made up of two letters, "n" and "g." When the "n" and "g" are beside each other they make the sound /ng/.

2. Give your child some examples of words that have the /ng/ sound, like ring, sting, song, long, bang.

3. Show your child the *Build it, Write it* activity page.

4. Explain to him that he will look at the picture in the first column, identify the picture, and read the word under the picture.

5. Now, ask your child to slowly and smoothly sound out the word. You can help him with this process. Once he sounds out the word, instruct him to look for the correct wooden letters to spell the word in the second column. Ask him to read the word.

6. After he has spelled the word in the second column, your child will move to the third column to write the word. After he has written the word, ask him to read it.

7. Repeat Steps 4-6 for the remaining pictures.

Lesson 11

Activity 2

MATERIALS:

☐ Chalk
☐ Squirt Bottle or Squirt Gun

DIRECTIONS:

1. Using chalk, go outside and write all of the New Words for Lesson 11 on the driveway or sidewalk.

2. Fill a squirt bottle or squirt gun with water.

3. Explain to your child that you will slowly sound out a word. He will then need to locate the written word on the driveway.

4. Once he locates the correct word, ask him to read the word.

5. Next, instruct your child to squirt the word with the squirt bottle or squirt gun until it washes away (this should be quite fun).

6. Continue until all words have been washed away.

● ● ●

Stories

Locate the Lesson 11 story titled "The Bird." Fold the story into a book. Ask your child to read the story to you as many times as he would enjoy.

Optional comprehension questions to ask your child:

1. What is the bird doing?

2. What happens while the bird is building a nest?

3. Is the bird sad about the storm? How do you know the bird is sad?

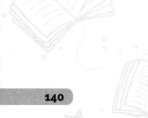

hung

lung

long

song

strong

bang

hang

king

wing

sing

finger

nothing

king		_____ - - - - - - - - - - - - _____
ring		_____ - - - - - - - - - - - - _____
fang		_____ - - - - - - - - - - - - _____
song		_____ - - - - - - - - - - - - _____
hang		_____ - - - - - - - - - - - - _____

cut along line

3

The nest must be strong.
sticks. He sings a song.
He starts to pick up

2

branch to form a nest.
The bird spots a long

A drip and drop hit the bird's
wing. The nest offers shelter
in the storm. During the
storm, the bird still sings.

4

The Bird

Lesson 11

1

Lesson 11

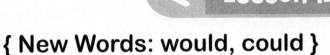

{ New Words: would, could }

Activity 1

MATERIALS:
- ☐ Paper
- ☐ White Crayon
- ☐ Washable Watercolor Paint
- ☐ Paintbrush

gab   dog

gut   hog

gap   bug

got   hug

bog   tug

DIRECTIONS:

1. On the piece of paper, use the white crayon to write sight words in random places. (Write the following sight words: would, could, said, too, other, where, want.)

2. Tell your child he will learn two new sight words today. Remind your child that sight words do not follow the rules for sounding out a word. Read the sight words on the *Flashcards* for Lesson 12 and ask your child to repeat the words. Practice the sight words several times with your child.

3. Explain to him that he is going to pretend to be a spy for this activity. There are secret hidden words on the piece of paper. He must use his special spy paint to uncover the hidden words.

4. Give your child a paintbrush, cup of water, and watercolor paints. Allow him to begin his spy discovery work.

5. When he uncovers a sight word, ask him to read the word.

6. Continue (Steps 4 and 5) until all sight words are uncovered and read.

Lesson 12

Stories

Locate the Lesson 12 story titled "Would You?" Fold the story into a book. Ask your child to read the story to you as many times as he would enjoy.

Show your children the question mark at the end of each sentence. Explain that this punctuation mark lets the reader know that a question has been asked.

Optional comprehension questions to ask your child:

1. Do you think this book was asking you to do real or silly things?

2. If you were to make a page in this book, what silly question would you include?

cut along line

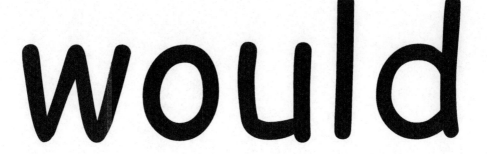

would

could

3

Would you or could you
pinch a burger?

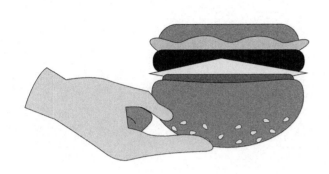

2

Would you or could you sing
a song during winter?

Would You?

Would you or could you
swim with a shark in a
scarf?

4

Lesson 12

1

{ New Words: bake, take, shake, save, game, flame, made, **}**
grape, late, whale, cane, safe

Bonus Flashcards included in printable appendix:

wake, cake, lake, make, fake, Jake, snake, flake, rake, wave, cave, Dave,
gave, brave, tame, same, name, came, ape, cape, shape, ate, Nate, Kate,
gate, skate, plate, state, trade, shade, tale, sale, scale, mane, tape,
mate, rate

Activity 1

MATERIALS:

☐ *Magic "e" Wand* Activity Page (Appendix P)
☐ Scissors
☐ Craft Stick
☐ Glue

DIRECTIONS:

1. Cut out the words and the star on the *Magic "e" Wand* activity page.

2. Glue the "e" star to the end of a craft stick.

3. Tell your child that he will learn a new sound today. The sound is /ā/, said "a." Tell him that this sound is called a long vowel sound. It is when the vowel says its name. The reason the new words have the sound /ā/ is because there is a magic "e" at the end of the words that makes the "a" say /ā/ and the "e" is silent.

4. Give your child some examples of words that have the /ā/ sound, like cake, snake, game, cape, whale, tape.

5. Show your child the "word strip" that has the word "cap" on it from the *Magic "e" Wand* activity page.

6. Ask your child to place his finger under the letters to sound out and read the word "cap."

7. Explain to him that the word "cap" has a short vowel sound, /ă/.

8. Now, he will do a magic trick. Ask him to pick up the "e" star wand and place it after the "p" in "cap."

9. Explain to him that the "e" is magic. It turns the "a" into a long vowel sound, /ā/, and the "e" remains silent. And now there is a new word.

10. Ask him to place his finger under the letters to try sounding out and reading the new word of "cape."

11. Repeat Steps 5-10 with all of the word strips.

Lesson 13

Activity 2

MATERIALS:

☐ *Long "a" Mapping* Activity Page (Appendix Q)
☐ Crayons

DIRECTIONS:

1. Explain to your child that he will be mapping out words today. Show him the mapping chart on the *Long "a" Mapping* activity page. Explain that he will use the chart to map the words listed under the chart.

2. Go over the chart with your child. Explain that when he finds a short vowel sound in a word, he will place a breve (little u) over the vowel in the word—no words will have a short vowel sound in this activity. When he sees a digraph (two letters that make one sound) in the word, he will draw a box around the digraph—there can be two digraphs in one word. You can show him the code for long vowel sounds—he will draw a blue, straight line over the vowel. For the silent "e" he will cross it out with a red slash.

3. Each code is color coded.

4. Ask him to look at the first word, "lake."

5. Ask him to sound out and read the word.

6. Ask him if he hears a short or long vowel. (He should hear a long "a" sound.) Ask him to draw a blue macron (straight line) over the "a."

7. Now, ask him to place his finger under the word to sound out the word again.

8. Ask your child if he heard the "e" at the end of the word or if it was silent. (It was silent.) He will need to cross the "e" out with a red crayon.

9. Ask him to read the word again.

10. Ask him if he sees a digraph in the word. There is not one in the word "lake."

11. Continue mapping the remaining nine words.

   Answer Key:
   1. lake- blue macron over "a," red slash over "e"
   2. wave- blue macron over "a," red slash over "e"
   3. same- blue macron over "a," red slash over "e"
   4. grape- blue macron over "a," red slash over "e"
   5. shape- blue macron over "a," red slash over "e," purple box around "sh"
   6. skate- blue macron over "a," red slash over "e"
   7. made- blue macron over "a," red slash over "e"
   8. whale- blue macron over "a," red slash over "e," purple box around "wh"
   9. plate- blue macron over "a," red slash over "e"
   10. trade- blue macron over "a," red slash over "e"

Activity 3

MATERIALS:

☐ *Flashcards*

DIRECTIONS:

1. Invite your child to have a friendly competition of reading war with you.

2. Using the *Flashcards* from all of the Lessons, you will compete to see who can read the most cards.

3. Gather the *Flashcards* in a stack. Explain to your child that he will have two chances to read each *Flashcard* correctly. If he reads it correctly in those two tries then he gets to keep the card.

4. However, if does not read the *Flashcard* correctly in two tries, then you get to read the card and keep it.

5. The player with the most cards at the end of the reading challenge wins. (I usually offer my children a small prize for winning, like a piece of candy, and of course they get to brag to everyone that they won.)

● ● ●

Stories

Locate the Lesson 13 story titled "Jake the Snake." Fold the story into a book. Ask your child to read the story to you as many times as he would enjoy.

On Page 3, the word "thrilled" is used in a sentence. Your child can sound out the word "thrill," however he has not been introduced to past tense words yet. This would be a good time to teach him by placing your finger over the "ed" in the word "thrilled." Allow him to sound out the word "thrill." Then uncover the "ed" and explain that when he sees "ed" at the end of a word it says /ed/, said "duh." Tell him that by adding "ed" to the end of words it means that the action happened in the past.

He may practice the /ed/ sound on Page 4 with the word "slithered."

Optional comprehension questions to ask your child:

1. What did Jake make?

2. Who is Jake taking the cake to?

3. Do you think Kate is a friend of Jake?

4. What did they do after they ate the cake?

bake

take

shake

save

game

flame

made

grape

late

whale

cane

safe

cut along line

sam

ap

cap

at

plat

stat

mad

man

e

can

tap

mat

rat

cut along line

Phonics Skills	Code	Example
short vowel	⌣	căt
long vowel	—	cāke
silent letters	/	bike̷
digraphs	☐	[th]at

lake   skate

wave   made

same   whale

grape   plate

shape   trade

3

Kate was thrilled. She gave Jake a plate and a fork.

2

Jake the snake made a cake to take to Kate.

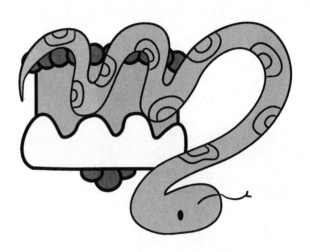

Lesson 13

Jake
the Snake

Jake and Kate ate the cake. Then Jake and Kate slithered to the lake for a swim.

4

Lesson 13

1

{ **New Words: hide, slide, like, chime, bite, quite, while, vine, shine, ripe, fire, drive** }

Bonus Flashcards included in printable appendix:

side, wide, ride, bride, hike, bike, time, dime, lime, kite, white, pile, smile, nine, pine, dine, line, mine, fine, wipe, pipe, stripe, tire, wire, dive, five, live

Activity 1

MATERIALS:

- ☐ *Magic "e" Pictures* Activity Page (Appendix R)
- ☐ White Crayon
- ☐ Washable Markers
- ☐ Scissors
- ☐ Glue

DIRECTIONS:

1. Explain to your child that he will learn a new sound today. The sound is /ī/, said "I." Tell him that this sound is called a long vowel sound. It is when the vowel says its name. The reason the new words have the sound /ī/ is because there is a magic "e" at the end of the words that makes the "i" say /ī/ and the "e" is silent.

2. Ask your child to practice reading some *Flashcards* for Lesson 14.

3. On the *Magic "e" Pictures* activity page, use the white crayon to secretly write a lowercase "e" on each blank.

4. Show your child the *Magic "e" Pictures* activity page. Explain to him that he will be a magician and make each word change into a new word.

5. Ask him to read the first word on the activity page, "dim."

6. Ask your child what kind of vowel sound is in the word "dim." (It is a short vowel sound.)

7. Now, ask your child to choose any color marker and color over the line after the word "dim."

8. Ask him what he sees. Explain that the "magic e" makes the short vowel sound in "dim" change to a long vowel sound and a new word.

9. Ask him to place his finger under the word to sound it out. The new word is "dime."

10. He can now look at the pictures at the bottom of the activity page to find a picture of a dime.

Lesson 14

11. Instruct him to cut out the dime and glue it next to the word "dime."

12. Repeat Steps 5-11 for the remaining words on the activity page.

• • •

Activity 2

MATERIALS:
☐ *Build a Sentence* Activity Page (Appendix S)
☐ Pencil

DIRECTIONS:

13. Show your child the *Build the Sentence* activity page.

14. Ask him to sound out and read each word in the word bank on the activity page.

15. Explain to him that he will read a sentence on the activity page and decide which word from the word bank would complete the sentence.

16. Ask your child to write the word in the blank and cross the word out in the word bank.

17. Complete the entire activity page together.

• • •

Stories

Locate the Lesson 14 story titled "Spring Time." Fold the story into a book. Ask your child to read the story to you as many times as he would enjoy.

Optional comprehension questions to ask your child:

1. What does the person in the story like to do in the spring?

2. What is the weather like in the spring?

3. What are your favorite things to do in the spring?

hide

slide

like

chime

bite

quite

while

vine

shine

ripe

fire

drive

cut along line

dim___		kit___	
pin___		bit___	
slid___		hid___	
tim___		rip ___	

wipe	tire	fire	bike	vine
chime	smile		white	

Pumpkins grow on a _____.

The car has a flat _____.

Get a rag to _____ up the mess.

I like to ride my _____.

Give a big _____ to the camera.

Hear the bells _____.

I want to cook hot dogs on the camp _____.

Pick up the _____ jacket and hang it up.

cut along line

3

The sun shines. I spot a kite.

2

I like spring time. I can go a hike. I can ride a bike.

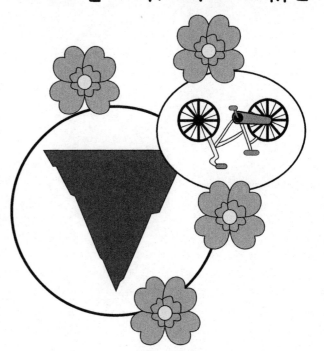

There are nine white buds starting to thrive. Spring is quite fun!

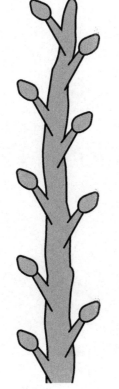

4

Spring Time

Lesson 14

1

Lesson 15

{ New Words: joke, smoke, hole, stole, home, bone, shone, }
rope, nose, close, chose

Bonus Flashcards included in printable appendix:

woke, broke, pole, Cole, dome, cone, stone, hope, slope, hose, rose

Activity 1

MATERIALS:

☐ *Short and Long "o" Game* Activity Page (Appendix T)
☐ Dice
☐ 2 Game Pieces

DIRECTIONS:

1. Tell your child that he will learn a new sound today. The sound is /ō/, said "o." Explain to your child that this sound is called a long vowel sound. It is when the vowel says its name. The reason the new words have the sound /ō/ is because there is a magic "e" at the end of the words that makes the "o" say /ō/ and the "e" is silent.

2. Give him some examples of words with a short "o" sound: cop, hop, pot, dog.

3. Give your child some examples of words with a long "o" sound: joke, bone, rope, close.

4. Show your child the *Short and Long "o" Game* activity page.

5. Explain to him that you will both place your game piece on the dog. The objective is to help the dog find his bone.

6. The first player will roll the dice and move his game piece the respective number of spaces.

7. He will then read the word in the spot his game piece landed. The player will identify if the word has a short or long "o" sound.

8. Player two will now take a turn following the same pattern.

9. The game will continue until one player reaches the bone first. He is the winner!

Activity 2

MATERIALS:

☐ Short and Long "o" Coloring Activity Page (Appendix U)
☐ Blue and Yellow Crayon

DIRECTIONS:

1. Show your child the *Short and Long "o" Coloring* activity page.

2. Explain to him that he will read each word on the activity page. Remind him to place his finger under the letters to sound out the words.

3. After he reads a word, he will decide if the word has a short or long "o" sound in the word. If the word has a /ŏ/ (short "o" sound) he will color the box blue. If the word has a /ō/ (long "o" sound) he will color the box yellow.

    Answer Key:
     not – blue
     joke – yellow
     dog – blue
     those – yellow
     note – yellow
     hot – blue
     woke – yellow
     pot – blue
     hope – yellow
     stole – yellow
     job – blue
     cone – yellow
     bog – blue
     rose – yellow
     zone – yellow
     jog – blue
     home – yellow
     rope – yellow
     slope – yellow
     nose – yellow
     hose – yellow
     shot – blue
     dome – yellow
     globe – yellow
     code – yellow

The Ultimate Teach Your Child to Read Activity Book: Developing Reader Autumn McKay

Stories

Locate the Lesson 15 story titled "The Hike." Fold the story into a book. Ask your child to read the story to you as many times as he would enjoy.

On Page 4, your child will be introduced to the apostrophe in "Cole's." Instruct your child that the word will read the same as if it did not have the apostrophe, so he would just add the /s/ sound at the end of the word "Cole." You can also tell him that this apostrophe shows ownership—Cole owns the hike.

Optional comprehension questions to ask your child:

1. Where is Cole going?

2. What does Cole do when he reaches the stone?

3. How does Cole avoid the hole?

cut along line

joke

smoke

hole

stole

home
bone
shone
rope

nose

close

chose

those

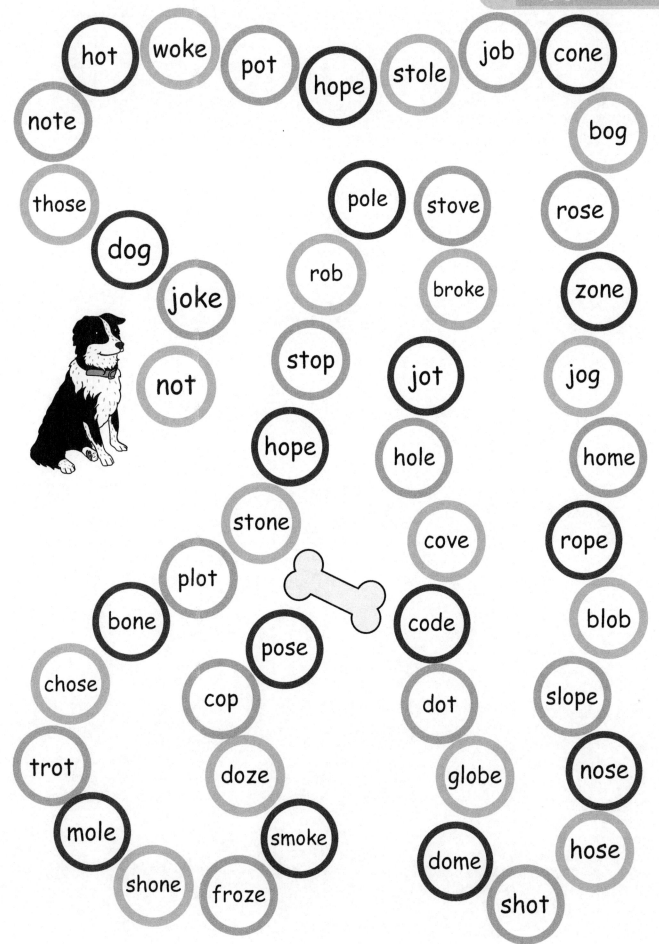

cut along line

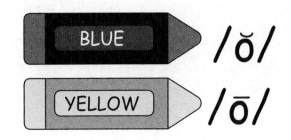

BLUE /ŏ/

YELLOW /ō/

not	joke	dog	those
note	hot	woke	pot
hope	stole	job	cone
bog	rose	zone	jog
home	rope	slope	nose
hose	shot	dome	globe

3

Cole comes to a stone. He climbs on top of the stone.

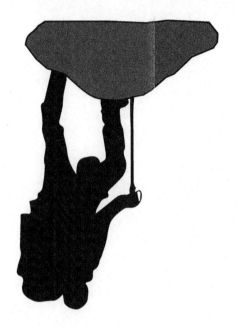

2

Cole will take a hike. Cole hikes up a big slope.

The Hike

Cole swings on the rope to miss the hole. After Cole's hike, he makes it home.

4

Lesson 15

1

cut along line

{ **New Words: use, rude, tune, dune, June, prune, flute, cute, tube, rule, mute** }

Activity 1

MATERIALS:

- ☐ Paper
- ☐ Marker
- ☐ 2 Large Bottle Caps
- ☐ Washable Paint
- ☐ Paper Plate

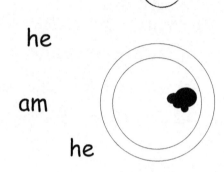

DIRECTIONS:

1. Explain to your child that he will learn a new sound today. The sound is /ū/, said "you." Tell him that this sound is called a long vowel sound. It is when the vowel says its name. The reason the new words have the sound /ū/ is because there is a magic "e" at the end of the words that makes the "u" say /ū/ and the "e" is silent.

2. Give your child some examples of words with a short "u" sound, /ŭ/: rug, bug, cub, duck, shut.

3. Give your child some examples of words with the long "u" sound, /ū/: cute, June, rude, flute, use.

4. On a sheet of paper, write all of the New Words (use, rude, tune, dune, June, prune, flute, cute, tube, rule, mute) and some short "u" words (stuck, shut, bug, mug, cut, puff, crust) in random order.

5. Select two colors of washable paint.

6. Squirt a dab of each color of washable paint on the paper plate.

7. Place one bottle cap in each color of paint.

8. Explain to your child that one color (Ex. red) will be for all words with a /ŭ/ (short "u" sound). The other color will be for all words with a /ū/ (long "u" sound).

9. Ask your child to select a word on the paper to read. After he has read the word, ask him to identify if the word had a /ŭ/ or /ū/ sound.

10. Use the appropriate bottle cap and paint color to stamp the word.

11. Continue until all words have been read and stamped.

Activity 2

MATERIALS:

☐ *Silent "e" Roll, Write, Read* Activity Page (Appendix V)
☐ Pencil
☐ Dice

DIRECTIONS:

1. Show your child the *Silent "e" Roll, Write, Read* activity page.

2. Instruct him that he will roll the dice.

3. Based on the number rolled, your child will look at the corresponding row of words. For example, if he rolls a four then he will look at the words "tun_, flut_, rul_, Jun_."

4. He will then write a lowercase "e" at the end of the first word. For the above example, he would write a lowercase "e" on the line at the end of "tun_."

5. He will then read the word.

6. Ask your child to roll the dice again and repeat Steps 3-5.

7. The object is to see which row of words will be completed first.

● ● ●

Stories

Locate the Lesson 16 story titled "The Flute." Fold the story into a book. Ask your child to read the story to you as many times as he would enjoy.

Optional comprehension questions to ask your child:

1. What is a flute?

2. Who is playing the flute?

3. Do you play or want to learn to play an instrument? What instrument?

4. Do you have to practice a lot to learn a new skill?

use

rude

tune

dune

cut along line

June

prune

flute

cute

tube

rule

mute

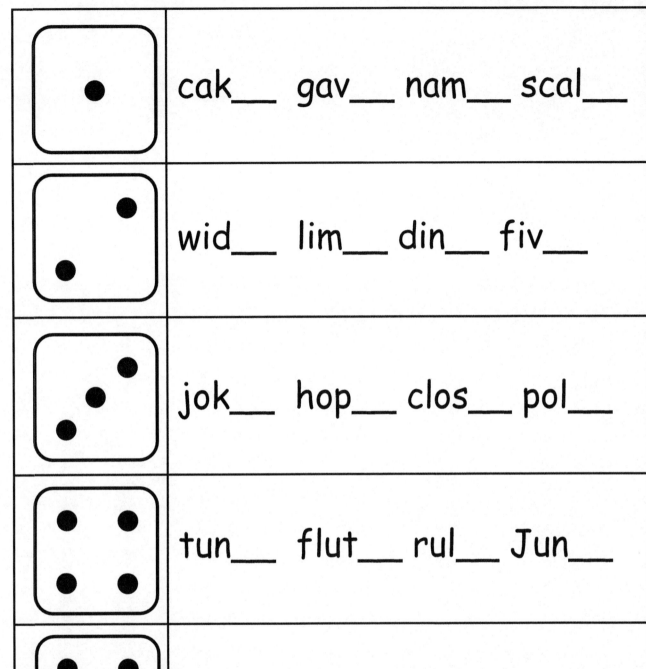	cak___ gav___ nam___ scal___
	wid___ lim___ din___ fiv___
	jok___ hop___ clos___ pol___
	tun___ flut___ rul___ Jun___
	saf___ shin___ chos___ mut___
	smok___ lik___ cut___ wav___

cut along line

3

She works hard with the flute.

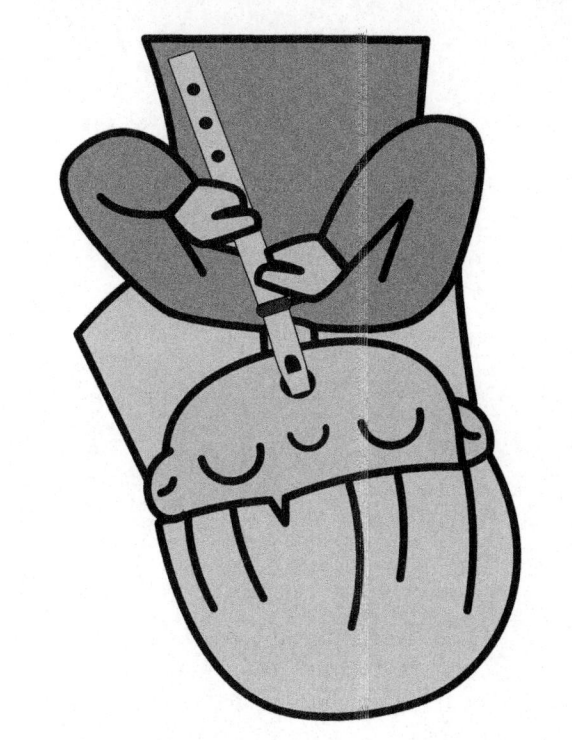

2

June likes the flute. June chose the flute.

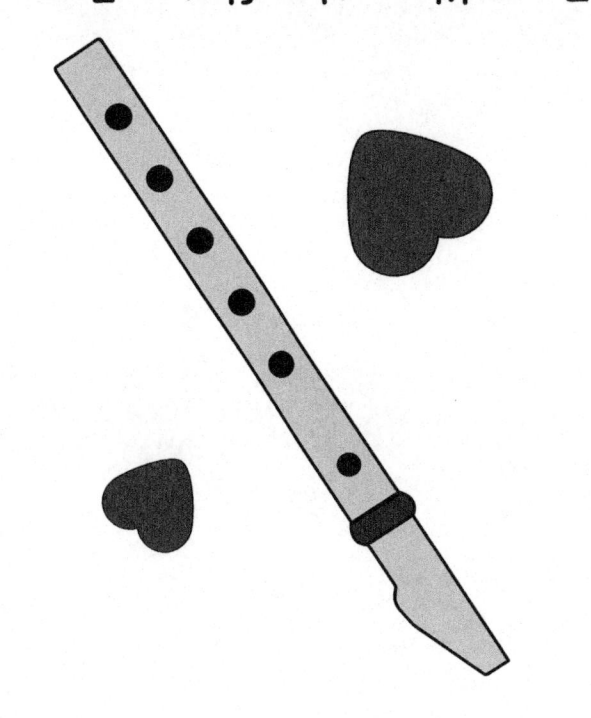

June makes a cute tune with the flute.

4

The Flute

Lesson 16

1

Lesson 16

{ New Words: should, know, they }

Activity 1

MATERIALS:

☐ *Color by Sight Word* Activity Page (Appendix W)
☐ Crayons

DIRECTIONS:

1. Tell your child that he will learn three new sight words today. Remind your child that sight words do not follow the rules for sounding out a word. Read the words on the Lesson 17 *Flashcards* to your child and ask him to repeat the words. Practice the new sight words with your child several times.

2. Show your child the *Color by Sight Word* activity page.

3. Ask him to read all seven sight words in the color code key at the top of the activity page.

4. Explain to your child that he will select a shape on the picture, read the word inside the shape, look at the color code key to determine what color to color the shape, and then color the shape.

5. Complete each shape to reveal the picture.

● ● ●

Stories

Locate the Lesson 17 story titled "The Big Test." Fold the story into a book. Ask your child to read the story to you as many times as he would enjoy.

Your child should be familiar with the sight word "come" and the digraph /ng/. On page 2, you will notice a variation of the word "come" as "coming." Assist your child as needed in reading the word "coming." (Please explain to him that when a word ends in an "e" he must remove the "e" to add an "ing." Please don't expect your child to fully grasp this rule yet. This is usually taught in first and second grade, but it is nice to introduce new rules.)

Optional comprehension questions to ask your child:

1. Who is taking a test?

2. What does Hope need to know for the test?

3. How did Hope do on the test?

should

know

they

cut along line

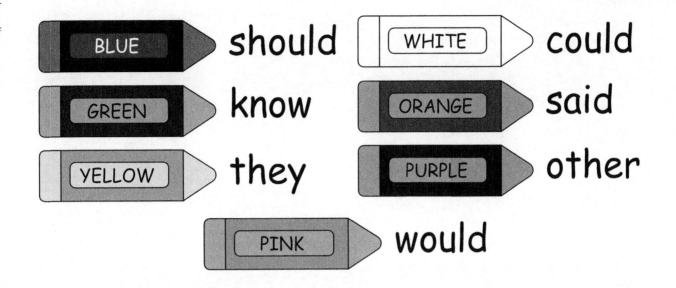

BLUE — should   WHITE — could

GREEN — know   ORANGE — said

YELLOW — they   PURPLE — other

PINK — would

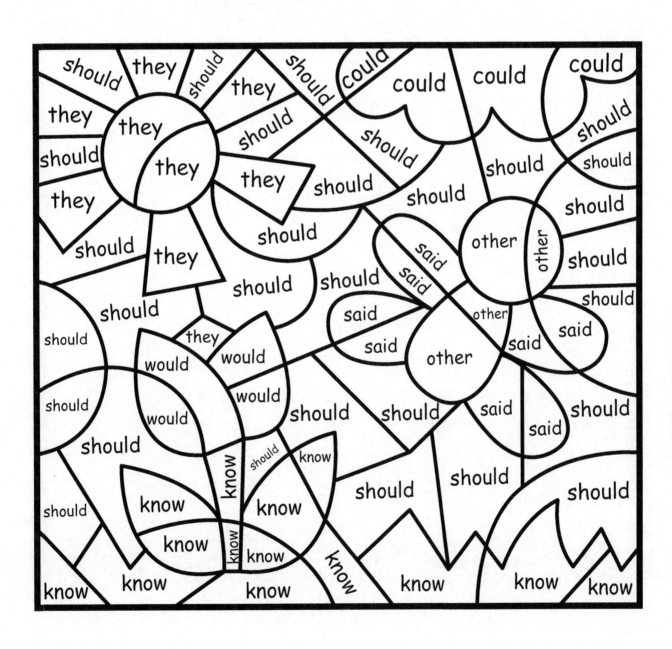

Lesson 17

3

She should know the name of the states.

2

Hope has a big test coming up. It is a test on states.

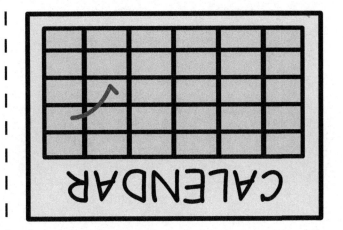

CALENDAR

The Big Test

Hope takes the test. She made a 100!

4

Lesson 17

1

{ **New Words: aim, main, pain, fair, sail, nail, chair, trail, paint, waiter, bay, play** }

Bonus Flashcards included in printable appendix:

air, aid, paid, gain, mail, wait, hair, pair, rain, laid, fail, rail, tail, jail, bait, pail, claim, chain, train, plain, grain, drain, snail, quail, may, way, day, lay, today, layer, gray, stay, subway

Activity 1

MATERIALS:

☐ *"ai" Mapping* Activity Page (Appendix X)
☐ Crayons

DIRECTIONS:

1. Tell your child that he has learned the /ā/ (long "a") sound in words with a magic "e," but there are more ways to form the /ā/ sound in words. In this lesson he will learn about two digraphs that make the /ā/ sound—"ai" and "ay." The digraph "ai" is usually found at the beginning or middle of words and the "ay" digraph is found at the end of words. This activity will focus on the "ai" digraph.

   When two vowels are beside each other in a word the first one does the talking and the second one does the walking. In the instance of "ai," the "a" says /ā/ and the "i" is silent. It's the same with "ay" since "y" is sometimes considered a vowel.

2. Practice reading a few *Flashcards* for Lesson 18 together. Remember to ask him to place his finger under the word to sound out the letters and digraphs.

3. Explain to your child that he will be mapping out words today.

4. Show him the mapping chart on the *"ai" Mapping* activity page. Explain that he will use the chart to map the words listed under the chart.

5. Go over the chart with your child. Explain that when he finds a short vowel sound in a word, he will place a breve (little u) over the vowel in the word (no words will have a short vowel sound in this activity). When he sees a digraph (two letters that make one sound) in the word, he will draw a purple box around the digraph (there can be two digraphs in one word). You can show him the code for long vowel sounds—he will draw a blue, straight line over the vowel. For the silent letter, he will cross it out with a red slash. It is acceptable to overlap codes.

6. Each code is color coded.

7. Ask your child to look at the first word, "nail."

8. Ask him to sound out and read the word.

9. Ask him if he sees a digraph in the word. He should locate the digraph "ai." He may draw a purple box around it.

10. Ask your child to read the word.

11. Ask him if he hears a short or long vowel. He should hear a long "a" sound. Ask him to draw a blue macron (straight line) over the "a."

12. Now, ask him to place his finger under the word to sound out the word again.

13. Ask your child to look at the digraph "ai." Ask him if he hears the "i" sound or if it is silent (It is silent). Ask him to make a red slash through the "i."

14. Ask him to read the word again.

15. Continue mapping the remaining seven words.

Answer Key:

1. nail- purple box around "ai," blue macron above "a," red slash through "i"

2. claim- purple box around "ai," blue macron above "a," red slash through "i"

3. paid- purple box around "ai," blue macron above "a," red slash through "i"

4. waiter- purple box around "ai" and "er," blue macron above "a," red slash through "i"

5. chain- purple box around "ai" and "ch," blue macron above "a," red slash through "i"

6. mail- purple box around "ai," blue macron above "a," red slash through "i"

7. rain- purple box around "ai," blue macron above "a," red slash through "i"

8. chair- purple box around "ai" and "ch," blue macron above "a," red slash through "i"

Activity 2

MATERIALS:

☐ *"ai" Decoder* Activity Page (Appendix Y)
☐ Pencil

DIRECTIONS:

1. Show your child the *"ai" Decoder* activity page.

2. Explain to him that he will have to be a detective to discover the "ai" words.

3. Ask your child to look at the first code "16-1-9-18." Explain to him that he will need to look in the decoder to find the letter that matches the number.

4. Ask him to locate the number 16 in the decoder.

5. Once he locates it, ask him to write the letter on the blank beside the code.

6. Now ask him to do the same for numbers 1, 9, and 18. It should reveal the word "pair."

7. After he has written each letter in the code, ask him to sound out and read the word.

8. Continue decoding the remaining nine words.

   Answer Key:
   1. pair
   2. mail
   3. train
   4. quail
   5. aim
   6. grain
   7. fair
   8. bait
   9. chair
   10. jail

Activity 3

MATERIALS:

- ☐ Post-It Notes
- ☐ Marker
- ☐ Fly Swatter

DIRECTIONS:

1. Ask your child to practice sounding out and reading the "ay" words for Lesson 18 using the *Flashcards*.

2. Write the "ay" words for Lesson 18 (may, say, bay, way, day, lay, play, clay, today, layer, gray, stay, subway) on Post-It Notes (one word per Post-It-Note).

3. Stick the Post-It Notes on the floor around the room.

4. Explain to your child that you will call out a word, and he must locate the correct word and hit it with the fly swatter.

5. Call out a word. Cheer him on as he locates the correct word.

6. Repeat Step 5 until all words have been swatted.

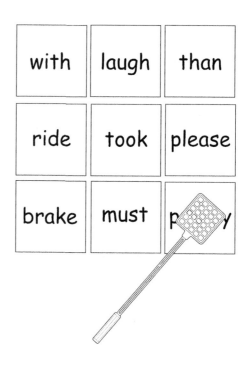

Activity 4

MATERIALS:

☐ *Long "a" Cupcakes* Activity Pages (Appendix Z)
☐ Crayons
☐ Scissors
☐ Tape

DIRECTIONS:

1. Ask your child to help you make a dice for this activity using the second page of the *Long "a" Cupcakes* activity page.

2. Cut out the template.

3. Fold the paper at each dotted line.

4. Fold the tabs under and tape the edges together to form a cube.

5. Show your child the first page of the *Long "a" Cupcakes* activity page.

6. Explain to your child that he will roll the dice to determine what kind of long "a" word to find on his cupcakes. For example, if the dice lands on "a_e" then he will locate a cupcake with a long "a" and silent "e."

7. Once your child locates the appropriate word, ask him to read the word on the cupcake.

8. Next, instruct your child to color the cupcake, matching the color of the cupcake on the dice. Cupcakes with "a_e" words should be colored blue, cupcakes with "ai" words should be colored yellow, and cupcakes with "ay" words should be colored pink.

9. Continue playing until all cupcakes are read and colored.

● ● ●

Stories

Locate the Lesson 18 story titled "The Train.." Fold the story into a book. Ask your child to read the story to you as many times as he would enjoy.

Optional comprehension questions to ask your child:

1. What color is the train?

2. Do you think it's hard for the train to drive in the rain?

3. What is the train's final destination?

Lesson 18

aim

main

pain

fair

cut along line

sail

nail

chair

trail

paint

waiter

bay

play

Phonics Skills	Code	Example
short vowel	‿	căt
long vowel	—	cāke
silent letters	/	bik/
digraphs	☐	t‌h‌at

nail   chain

claim   mail

paid   rain

waiter   chair

a	b	c	d	e	f	g	h	i	j	k	l	m
1	2	3	4	5	6	7	8	9	10	11	12	13

n	o	p	q	r	s	t	u	v	w	x	y	z
14	15	16	17	18	19	20	21	22	23	24	25	26

16-1-9-18

13-1-9-12

20-18-1-9-14

17-21-1-9-12

1-9-13

7-18-1-9-14

6-1-9-18

2-1-9-20

3-8-1-9-18

10-1-9-12

cut along line

take

tail

day

play

cake

sail

cape

grain

may

mate

aid

gray

plate

snail

way

flame

wait

game

3

2

It starts to rain. The gray
train still chugs.

The gray train drives on
the rails. It must take the
mail to the next stop.

It makes its way to the
subway stop. The gray
train made it!

The Train

cut along line

{ **New Words: eat, each, read, wheat, keep, three, sheep, fifteen, key, sunny, party, be** }

Bonus Flashcards included in printable appendix:

sea, ear, year, real, team, mean, lead, near, east, hear, deal, seat, beat, bear, wear, heat, weak, peak, jeans, meat, meal, gear, leap, leaf, neat, leak, pea, reach, learn, speak, least, clean, dream, teach, beach, steam, cream, cheap, feast, beast, sneak, scream, peanut, see, need, week, free, seen, meet, feel, feet, deep, seem, feed, tree, seed, beef, weed, jeep, beep, speed, sheet, green, sleep, queen, sweet, sweep, creek, street, screen, seeing, between, sixteen, wheel, money, hockey, turkey, jersey, monkey, donkey, any, only, many, very, easy, body, copy, busy, lily, story, every, daily, happy, fifty, empty, sixty, dirty, silly, lucky, daddy, mommy, really, pretty, thirty, he, she, we, me

Activity 1

MATERIALS:

☐ *Flashcards* for Lesson 19
☐ Post-It Notes
☐ Marker
☐ Object for Each Long "e" Sound

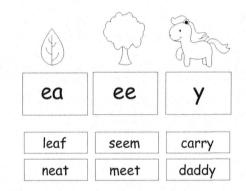

DIRECTIONS:

1. Tell your child that he will learn the long "e" sound, /ē/, said "e." There are five different digraphs or ways to form the /ē/ sound— "ea" as in the word "leaf," "ee" as in the word "jeep," "ey" as in the word "money," "y" as in the word "story," and "e" as in the word "me."

   When two vowels are beside each other in a word the first one does the talking and the second one does the walking. In the instance of "ea," the "e" says /ē/ and the "a" is silent. It's the same with "ey" since "y" is sometimes considered a vowel.

2. Practice reading a few *Flashcards* for Lesson 19 together. Remember to ask him to place his finger under the word to sound out the letters and digraphs.

3. Locate an item from around your house for the "ea," "ee," "ey," and "y" digraph groups. For example, you can select a "leaf" or "bead" for the "ea" digraph. You might select a "seed" or something "green" for the "ee" digraph.

4. On one Post-It Note write the digraph "ea" in lowercase letters.

5. Place the Post-It Note on the floor.

6. Place the "ea" household item above the Post-It Note.

7. On the second Post-It Note write the digraph "ee" in lowercase letters.

8. Place the Post-It Note six inches away from the "ea" Post-It Note.

9. Set the "ee" household item above the "ee" Post-It Note.

10. On the third Post-It Note write the "ey" digraph in lowercase letters.

11. Place the Post-It Note six inches away from the "ee" Post-It Note.

12. Set the "ey" household item above the "ey" Post-It Note.

13. On the fourth Post-It Note write the "y" digraph in a lowercase letter.

14. Place the Post-It Note six inches away from the "ey" Post-It Note.

15. Set the "y" household item above the "y" Post-It Note.

16. Shuffle the *Flashcards* for Lesson 19.

17. Allow your child to choose a *Flashcard*. Ask your child to read the word on the *Flashcard* by sounding it out.

18. Now ask your child to determine with which Post-It Note digraph group the *Flashcard* belongs—"ea, ee, ey, y."

19. Ask him to place the *Flashcard* under the correct Post-It Note.

20. Repeat Steps 17-19 until all *Flashcards* are sorted. There are many *Flashcards* for Lesson 19, so this activity can be completed over several days.

The Ultimate Teach Your Child to Read Activity Book: Developing Reader Autumn McKay

Activity 2

MATERIALS:

- ☐ *Glue Tracing* Activity Pages (Appendix AA)
- ☐ Liquid Glue
- ☐ Glitter (Optional)

DIRECTIONS:

1. Present your child with the *Glue Tracing* activity pages.

2. Explain to him that he will place his index finger under the letters to say the sound of the letter or digraph, and then slide his finger under the word as he blends the sounds together to read the word.

3. After he reads one word, allow him to use the liquid glue to trace the letters of the word.

4. If he would like, he can sprinkle glitter over the glue. (As pretty as glitter is to the object it decorates, it often creates a significant mess, consider some creative options and let me know by email what your child used).

5. Repeat Steps 2-4 for the remaining words on the activity pages.

Activity 3

MATERIALS:

- ☐ 2 Sets of the "ee" *Flashcards* for Lesson 19 in Different Colors
- ☐ Scissors

DIRECTIONS:

1. Present your child with the *Glue Tracing* activity pages.

Activity 3

MATERIALS:

☐ 2 Sets of the "ee" *Flashcards* for Lesson 19 in Different Colors
☐ Scissors

DIRECTIONS:

1. Print two sets of the "ee" *Flashcards* for Lesson 19 (see, need, week, keep, free, seen, meet, feel, feet, deep, seem, feed, tree, seed, beef, weed, jeep, sheep, beep, three, speed, sheet, green, sleep, queen, sweet, sweep, creek, street, screen, seeing, between, fifteen, sixteen, wheel). Each set needs to be a different color, so one set can be printed on white cardstock and the other on yellow cardstock.

2. Cut out all *Flashcards*.

3. Put one set of *Flashcards* (the color set) in a pile face down between the two players.

4. Next, give each player six cards from the other set of *Flashcards* (the white set). Put the remaining (white) cards in a pile separate from the color set and place them face down.

5. Start with the youngest player. He will turn over a color card and read the word on the card.

6. Both players will check their six white cards to see if one player has the same word as the one on the color card.

7. If a player has the matching card, then he will get to keep the matching set and take another card from the white set so that the player continues to have six cards in his hand.

8. If no one has the matching card in their hand then turn the next color card over. If the turned over card has a match the player will only take the card that has a match, but not any previous cards.

9. The game will continue until all color cards have been turned over.

10. The player with the largest number of matches wins.

The Ultimate Teach Your Child to Read Activity Book: Developing Reader Autumn McKay

Activity 4

MATERIALS:

☐ *Read and Highlight* Activity Page (Appendix AB)
☐ Highlighter

DIRECTIONS:

1. Show your child the *Read and Highlight* activity page.

2. Explain to him that he will read a sentence on the activity page. As he hears a word with a /ē/ (long "e" sound) he will use the highlighter to highlight the word.

3. Complete the activity page.

4. After he has read each sentence and highlighted all of the /ē/ words, ask him to go back and read all of the highlighted words.

• • •

Stories

Locate the Lesson 19 story titled "At the Beach." Fold the story into a book. Ask your child to read the story to you as many times as he would enjoy.

You will notice two words in this story that are highlighted green and orange ("seaweed" and "seashells"). Explain to your child that these are compound words (two words that combine to make one word). To help your child read compound words instruct him to read the green word first, then the orange word, and then combine the words to make one word.

Optional comprehension questions to ask your child:

1. Who goes to the beach?

2. What does Lily do when seaweed touches her feet?

3. How many seashells did Steve collect?

4. What is your favorite thing to do at the beach?

eat

each

read

wheat

keep

three

sheep

fifteen

key

sunny

party

be

cut along line

sea

each

read

bear

learn

teach

feast

peanut

wheat

jeans

Read the sentences.
Highlight the long e words.

1. She has a peach seed.
2. The monkey sips water from the creek.
3. The queen wears a pretty ring.
4. He sees a sheep in a jeep.
5. The leaf on the tree is very green.
6. I like have sweet dreams.

3

Lily screams when seaweed meets her feet. Steve collects sixteen seashells.

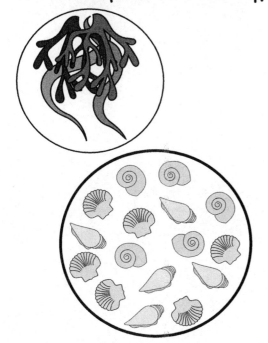

2

Lily and Steve spend a sunny day at the beach. They jump in the sea.

At the Beach

They had a busy day. Lily and Steve are happy they went to the beach.

4

Lesson 19

1

{ **New Words: oak, boat, goal, soak, coach, board, throat, mow, show, yellow, rainbow, no** }

Bonus Flashcards included in printable appendix:

oat, road, load, coal, soap, coat, goat, toad, coast, toast, roast, float, own, row, tow, low, bow, flow, snow, crow, glow, slow, blow, below, throw, elbow, follow, window, shadow, borrow, hollow, so, go

Activity 1

MATERIALS:

☐ *Playdough Long "o" Reading* Activity Page (Appendix AC)
☐ Playdough

DIRECTIONS:

1. Tell your child that he will learn the long "o" sound, /ō/, said "oh." There are three different digraphs or ways to form the /ō/ sound—"oa" as in the word "boat," "ow" as in the word "row," and "o" as in the word "no."

   Remind your child that when two vowels are beside each other in a word the first one does the talking and the second one does the walking. In the instance of "oa," the "o" says /ō/ and the "a" is silent.

2. Practice reading a few *Flashcards* for Lesson 20 together. Remember to ask your child to place his finger under the word to sound out the letters and digraphs.

3. Show your child the *Playdough Long "o" Reading* activity page.

4. Ask your child to help you make little balls of playdough to fit in each blue circle on the activity page.

5. Place each playdough ball on the blue circles.

6. Explain to your child that he will sound out the words on the activity page by pressing the playdough ball flat with his finger and saying the sound of the letter or letters in the box above the playdough.

   For instance, for the word "road," your child will flatten the first playdough ball with his index finger and say /r/. Then he will flatten the second playdough ball and say /ō/. Lastly, he will flatten the third playdough ball and say /d/.

7. Then he will slide his finger under the word to combine all sounds into a word.

   Using the example above he would slide his finger under the word and say "road."

8. Ask your child to read each word on the activity page.

Activity 2

MATERIALS:

☐ *Long "o" Tic-Tac-Toe* Activity Page (Appendix AD)
☐ Pom Poms
☐ *Flashcards* (goat, toad, soap, toast, rainbow, snow, bow, shadow, blow)

DIRECTIONS:

1. Gather the following *Flashcards*—goat, toad, soap, toast, rainbow, snow, bow, shadow, blow.

2. Shuffle the *Flashcards*. Place them face down.

3. Invite your child to play a game of tic-tac-toe with you using the *Long "o" Tic-Tac-Toe* activity page.

4. You will each need to choose a different color pom pom. Get five pom poms of the color you picked.

5. Instruct your child that to play this game he will need to flip over a *Flashcard*, read the word on the *Flashcard*, find the corresponding picture on the activity page, and place his pom pom on the picture.

6. The next player will repeat the same process as directed in Step 5.

7. The first player to place three *Flashcards* in a row vertically, horizontally, or diagonally wins.

8. Play as many times as your child would enjoy.

• • •

Activity 3

MATERIALS:

☐ *Long "o" Clues* Activity Page (Appendix AE)
☐ Pencil

DIRECTIONS:

1. Show your child the *Long "o" Clues* activity page.

2. Explain to him that he will be a detective today. He will read the clue in the box and try to determine the mystery word or spelling of a word.

3. He may use *Flashcards* for Lesson 20 if he needs help in figuring out some of the answers to the clues.

4. Assist your child in reading the clues if he needs help, but please let him try to solve the clues himself. However, if he is struggling you may prompt him to find the answer himself.

The Ultimate Teach Your Child to Read Activity Book: Developing Reader Autumn McKay

Stories

Locate the Lesson 20 story titled "The Coat.". Fold the story into a book. Ask your child to read the story to you as many times as he would enjoy.

Optional comprehension questions to ask your child:

1. Who stole the coat?

2. Where did the goat take the coat?

3. Do you think this story is real or pretend?

oak

boat

goal

soak

coach

board

throat

mow

show

yellow

rainbow

no

cut along line

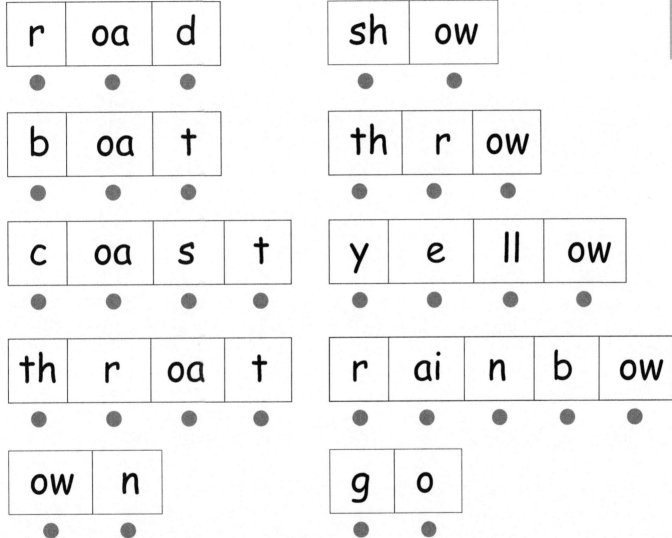

r	oa	d
sh	ow
b	oa	t
th	r	ow
c	oa	s	t
y	e	ll	ow
th	r	oa	t
r	ai	n	b	ow
ow	n
g	o

cut along line

What word rhymes with coat and starts with a "b"? _____	Which word is spelled correctly? snoa snow 	What two letters complete the word? wind_ _
How many letters are in the word below?  3 or 4	Write the missing letters. elb__ __ 	What word rhymes with tow and starts with an "m"?  _____
Which word is spelled correctly? toast towst 	How many letters are in the word below?  _____	Which word is spelled correctly? yellow yelloa

3

The goat stole the coat.
He ran up the road with
the coat.

2

I went to the farm and met
a goat. The goat was eating
oats.

The Coat

I must follow the goat to
get the coat. He takes
the coat to a crow.

4

Lesson 20

1

{ New Words: one, two }

Activity 1

MATERIALS:

☐ *Bean Toss* Activity Page (Appendix AF)
☐ Dried Beans
☐ Muffin Pan

DIRECTIONS:

1. Tell your child he will learn two new sight words today. Remind your child that sight words do not follow the rules for sounding out a word. Read the words on the *Flashcards* to your child and ask him to repeat the words (do this several times).

2. Cut out the circles on the *Bean Toss* activity page.

3. Insert the cut-outs in the muffin pan cups (one cut-out per cup).

4. Explain to your child that you will give him some dried beans. Ask him to stand six feet from the muffin pan. (Adjust distance closer if needed).

5. Now ask your child to toss one bean towards the muffin pan.

6. If the bean lands inside a muffin pan cup, then your child will read the sight word in the cup. If the bean does not land inside a muffin pan cup, allow him to toss another bean.

7. See if your child can toss a bean inside each muffin pan cup.

● ● ●

Stories

Locate the Lesson 21 story titled "Rocks." Fold the story into a book. Ask your child to read the story to you as many times as he would enjoy.

Optional comprehension questions to ask your child:

1. Do you like to collect rocks?

2. How many rocks did the child collect?

one

two

cut along line

one two should

know they would

could said too

other where want

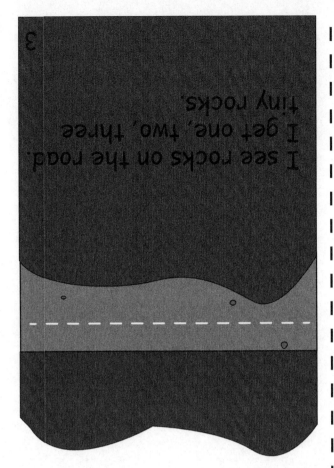

I see rocks on the road.
I get one, two, three
tiny rocks.

3

I like rocks. I see rocks at
the river. I get one, two,
three pretty rocks.

2

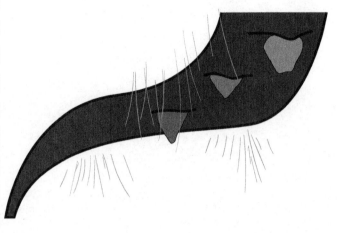

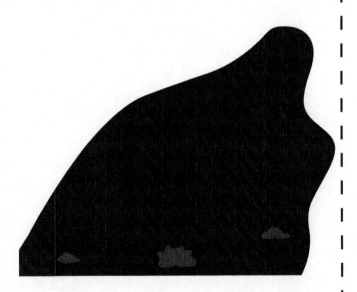

I spot rocks in a shadow.
I get one, two, three
bumpy rocks.

4

Rocks

Lesson 21

1

{ **New Words: tie, pie, by, my, fly, cry, spy, high, light, might, bright, thigh** }

Bonus Flashcards included in printable appendix:

die, lie, try, sky, dry, guy, shy, fry, why, sigh, night, right, fight, sight, tight, flight

Activity 1

MATERIALS:

☐ *Long "i" I-Spy* Activity Page (Appendix AG)
☐ Crayons

DIRECTIONS:

1. Tell your child that he will learn the long "i" sound, /ī/, said "eye." There are three different digraphs or ways to form the /ī/ sound—"ie" as in the word "pie," "y" as in the word "cry," and "igh" as in the word "high."

   (Remember the phrase and teach it to your child: When two vowels are beside each other in a word the first one does the talking and the second one does the walking. In the instance of "ie," the "i" says /ī/ and the "e" is silent.)

2. Practice reading the *Flashcards* for Lesson 22 together. Remember to ask your child to place his finger under the word to sound out the letters and digraphs.

3. Show your child the *Long "i" I-Spy* activity page.

4. Ask your child to read a word at the bottom of the activity page.

5. Next, ask your child to locate the word's corresponding picture.

6. Once your child locates the correct picture, he can color the picture and put a check mark next to the word.

7. Continue working until all words and pictures are matched.

Activity 2

MATERIALS:

☐ *Ice Cream Maze* Activity Page (Appendix AH)
☐ Pencil

DIRECTIONS:

1. Show your child the *Ice Cream Maze* activity page.

2. Explain to him that he needs to help the two friends get to their ice cream before it melts. Tell your child that to assist the two friends he must make his way through the maze. In his journey across the maze, when he comes to a word, he must read the word in order to continue through the maze

3. Cheer your child on as he travels through the maze.

● ● ●

Activity 3

MATERIALS:

☐ *Right Word* Activity Page (Appendix AI)
☐ Pencil

DIRECTIONS:

1. Show your child the *Right Word* activity page.

2. Instruct him to look at the picture and read the two words below the picture.

3. After he has read the words, ask him to identify which word best describes the picture. Color in the circle.

4. Complete the activity page.

● ● ●

Stories

Locate the Lesson 22 story titled "The Night Sky." Fold the story into a book. Ask your child to read the story to you as many times as he would enjoy.

Optional comprehension questions to ask your child:

1. Have you ever watched the stars at night?

2. What does the child spot in the sky?

3. Why do you think the child sighed as he watched the night sky?

tie

pie

by

my

fly

cry

spy

light

might

bright

thigh

tie ☐ pie ☐

fly ☐ light ☐

night ☐ flight ☐

right ☐ sky ☐

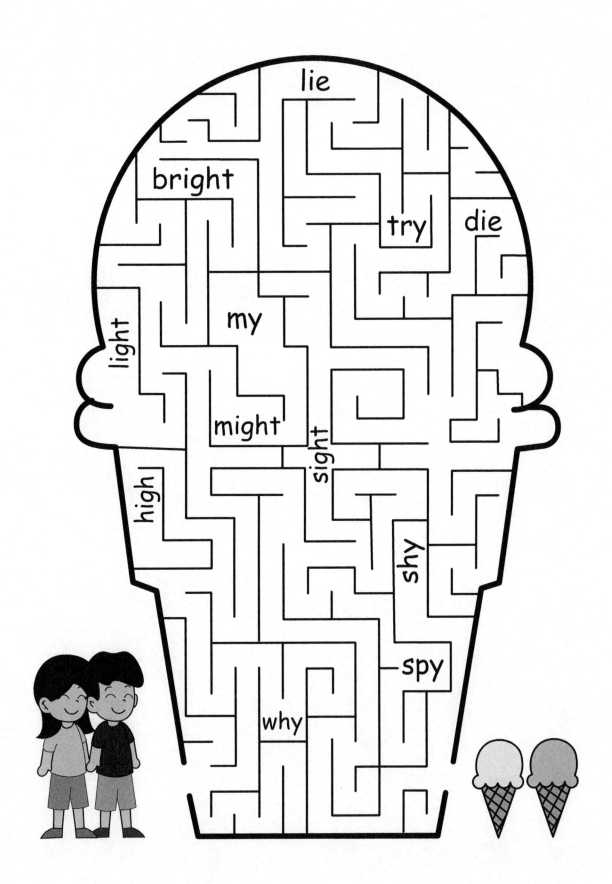

cut along line

cut along line

tie   fry
○   ○

bright   light
○   ○

sight   cry
○   ○

spy   sigh
○   ○

fly   flight
○   ○

might   night
○   ○

Lesson 22

3

The bright stars light up
the sky. I spot a star fly
by.

2

The night sky is very big. I
see many stars.

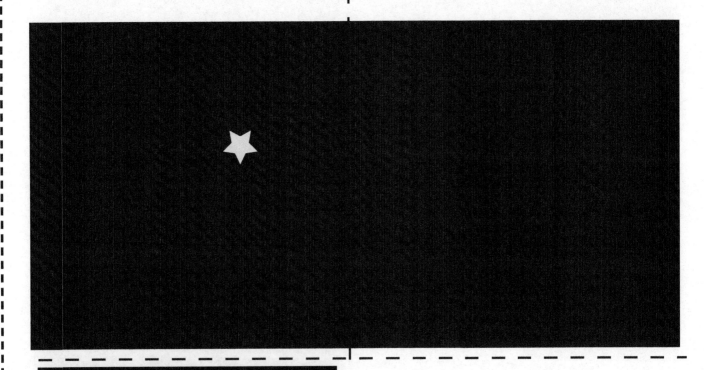

As I lie and watch the
night sky, I sigh.

4

Lesson 22

**The Night
Sky**

Lesson 22

1

{ **New Words: due, true, blue, argue, statue, suit, fruit, guitar, new, crew, threw, screw** }

Bonus Flashcards included in printable appendix:

sue, clue, glue, value, issue, rescue, tissue, fuel, fluid, few, drew, blew, grew, flew, chew

Activity 1

MATERIALS:

☐ *Flashcards* for Lesson 23
☐ Objects From Around the House

DIRECTIONS:

1. Tell your child that he will learn the long "u" sound, /ū/, said "yew." There are three different digraphs or ways to form the /ū/ sound—"ue" as in the word "blue," "ui" as in the word "fruit," and "ew" as in the word "new."

   (Can you say this with me: When two vowels are beside each other in a word the first one does the talking and the second one does the walking. In the instance of "ue," the "u" says /ū/ and the "e" is silent.)

2. Practice reading the *Flashcards* for Lesson 23 together. (Remember to ask your child to place his finger under the word to sound out the letters and digraphs.)

3. Cut out the *Flashcards* for Lesson 23: due, sue, true, blue, clue, glue, value, issue, argue, rescue, statue, tissue, fuel, suit, fruit, fluid, guitar, new, few, crew, drew, blew, grew, flew, chew, threw, screw.

4. Create an obstacle course in your home for your child. Here are some examples (from Lesson 9) of obstacles to include:

   1. Hop from pillow to pillow.

   2. Crawl under a table.

   3. Climb a mountain of pillows.

   4. Zoom a toy car along a piece of tape.

   5. Walk backwards around an island.

   6. Army crawl under a row of chairs.

   As you create the obstacle course, place *Flashcards* throughout the course.

5. Explain to your child that he will need to complete the obstacle course, but as he is working his way through the obstacle course, he will find cards with words that he must read before moving forward.

6. Cheer him on as he makes his way through the course.

• • •

Activity 2

MATERIALS:

- ☐ *Reading Battleship* Activity Pages (Appendix AJ)
- ☐ 2 File Folders
- ☐ Tape
- ☐ Crayons

DIRECTIONS:

1. Gather all four *Reading Battleship* activity pages. All pages are the same.

2. Open one of the file folders so that it is sitting in front of you like an open laptop.

3. Tape one *Reading Battleship* activity page to the bottom of the file folder. Tape the second *Reading Battleship* activity page to the top ("screen" portion of the laptop) of the file folder.

	1	2	3	4	5	6
A	shut	your	stop	grand	shark	mash
B	dark	pop	do	tub	dish	start
C	cash	hush	car	red	glad	hats
D	cups	bump	kick	mom	not	plan
E	truck	be	can	marsh	rash	flip
F	ran	add	pants	flush	stand	bed
G	hit	wet	six	pack	web	barn

	1	2	3	4	5	6
A	shut	your	stop	grand	shark	mash
B	dark	pop	do	tub	dish	start
C	cash	hush	car	red	glad	hats
D	cups	bump	kick	mom	not	plan
E	truck	be	can	marsh	rash	flip
F	ran	add	pants	flush	stand	bed
G	hit	wet	six	pack	web	barn

4. Repeat Steps 2 and 3 with the second file folder.

5. Sit opposite of your child so you cannot see his board and he cannot see your board. Keep the file folders in the "laptop" position.

6. Instruct your child to use his crayon to place his ships on his lower board (the one on the table). He will need to circle a row of 2 words, a row of 3 words, a row of 4 words, and a row of 5 words. He may circle them horizontally or vertically. He will have a total of four ships.

7. You will need to circle your ships on your lower board, as well.

8. Once you both have your ships circled, Player 1 (your child) will begin by calling out the coordinates (letter, number) and reading the word associated with the coordinate.

   For example, A, 1 = "true."

9. If Player 2's ship is not on the word Player 1 called out, then Player 2 will say, "miss." Player 1 will put an "X" on the coordinate he called out on the upper board ("screen" portion of the board) to help him remember that a ship is not in that location.

10. If Player 2's ship is on the word Player 1 called out, then Player 2 will say, "hit." Player 2 will color in the coordinate/word on the lower board that Player 1 called. Player 1 will color in the coordinate/word on the upper board that he called, so he will know to call another coordinate beside the "hit" ship.

11. Player 2 will take a turn following the same rules in Steps 8-10.

12. A player's ship is sunk once all spots circled are colored in.13. The winner is the first one to sink all of the other player's ships.

• • •

Stories

Locate the Lesson 23 story titled "The Clue." Fold the story into a book. Ask your child to read the story to you as many times as he would enjoy.

Optional comprehension questions to ask your child:

1. What clue does the child find?

2. Where did he find the clue?

3. Where does the clue lead the child?

cut along line

due

true

blue

argue

statue

suit

fruit

guitar

new

crew

threw

screw

	1	2	3	4	5	6
A	true	lie	fuel	team	guitar	threw
B	own	blue	by	suit	stay	new
C	sue	so	clue	screw	fruit	mail
D	paint	issue	he	glue	high	fluid
E	few	today	argue	any	value	oak
F	copy	crew	leak	rescue	key	due
G	grew	we	drew	beep	statue	seen
H	chew	flew	soak	blew	hockey	tissue

	1	2	3	4	5	6
A	true	lie	fuel	team	guitar	threw
B	own	blue	by	suit	stay	new
C	sue	so	clue	screw	fruit	mail
D	paint	issue	he	glue	high	fluid
E	few	today	argue	any	value	oak
F	copy	crew	leak	rescue	key	due
G	grew	we	drew	beep	statue	seen
H	chew	flew	soak	blew	hockey	tissue

cut along line

cut along line

	1	2	3	4	5	6
A	true	lie	fuel	team	guitar	threw
B	own	blue	by	suit	stay	new
C	sue	so	clue	screw	fruit	mail
D	paint	issue	he	glue	high	fluid
E	few	today	argue	any	value	oak
F	copy	crew	leak	rescue	key	due
G	grew	we	drew	beep	statue	seen
H	chew	flew	soak	blew	hockey	tissue

cut along line

	1	2	3	4	5	6
A	true	lie	fuel	team	guitar	threw
B	own	blue	by	suit	stay	new
C	sue	so	clue	screw	fruit	mail
D	paint	issue	he	glue	high	fluid
E	few	today	argue	any	value	oak
F	copy	crew	leak	rescue	key	due
G	grew	we	drew	beep	statue	seen
H	chew	flew	soak	blew	hockey	tissue

3

There is a clue by the guitar. What is it? It is a blue screw.

2

I am a spy. I seek new clues.

This clue leads me to my dad. I know he will help me turn up a few new clues.

4

The Clue

Lesson 23

1

{ **New Words: too, boo, zoo, mood, food, tool, pool, cool, stool, spool, room, zoom** }

Bonus Flashcards included in printable appendix:

broom, bloom, soon, noon, moon, spoon

Activity 1

MATERIALS:

☐ *Fruit Loop Words* Activity Page (Appendix AK)
☐ Fruit Loops

DIRECTIONS:

1. Tell your child that he will learn the digraph "oo." This digraph makes two different sounds. Today you will focus on the long "oo" sound, /u:/, it makes, said "ew."

2. Practice reading the *Flashcards* for Lesson 24 together. Remember to ask your child to place his finger under the word to sound out the letters and digraphs.

3. Show him the *Fruit Loop Words* activity page.

4. Hand him a bowl of fruit loops.

5. Ask him to look at the first word on the activity page, "t_ _."

6. Ask him to place a fruit loop on each blank.

7. Now, he will place his finger under the word and sound out the letters/digraph to read the word. Remind him that "oo" says "ew."

8. Continue Steps 5-7 for the rest of the activity page.

9. He may enjoy a snack of Fruit Loops when he completes the activity page.

Stories

Locate the Lesson 24 story titled "At the Zoo." Fold the story into a book. Ask your child to read the story to you as many times as he would enjoy.

Optional comprehension questions to ask your child:

1. Where does the child go?

2. What does the child get to do at the zoo?

3. What is your favorite animal to see at the zoo?

too

boo

zoo

mood

food

tool

pool

cool

stool

spool

room

zoom

cut along line

t ___ ___

sp ___ ___ l

z ___ ___

r ___ ___ m

m ___ ___ d

z ___ ___ m

f ___ ___ d

br ___ ___ m

t ___ ___ l

bl ___ ___ m

p ___ ___ l

s ___ ___ n

c ___ ___ l

n ___ ___ n

st ___ ___ l

m ___ ___ n

sp ___ ___ n

I stand on a stool to feed the monkey food.

MONKEY FOOD

I go to the zoo at noon. At the zoo I see a monkey.

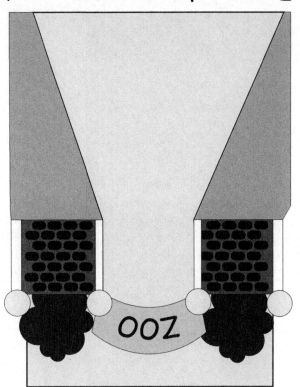

ZOO

Lesson 24

It is very cool! I want to go back soon.

At the Zoo

cut along line

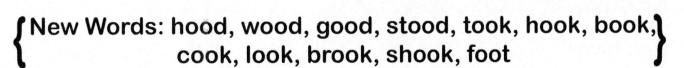

{ **New Words: hood, wood, good, stood, took, hook, book, cook, look, brook, shook, foot** }

Activity 1

MATERIALS:

☐ *"oo" Glasses* Activity Page (Appendix AL)
☐ *Flashcards* for Lesson 25

DIRECTIONS:

1. Tell your child that he will learn the digraph "oo." This digraph makes two different sounds. Today you will focus on the short "oo" sound, //, it makes, said "uh," like in the word "look." Go over a few more examples of // (short "oo" words) using the *Flashcards* for Lesson 25.

2. Show your child the *"oo" Glasses* activity page.

3. Help your child assemble the glasses.

4. Explain to your child that these glasses will help him look for and spot words with the short "oo" sound, //.

5. Ask your child to close his eyes. While his eyes are closed, hide the *Flashcards* for Lesson 24 and 25 around the room.

6. Ask your child to open his eyes. Now, he will use his special glasses to spot any // (short "oo" words). This will be tricky, so remind him that short "oo" words make the //, said "uh."

7. Once he finds a word, ask your child to sound it out to discover if the word has a long /u:/ or short // sound.

8. If it has a short "oo" sound, //, ask your child to bring the card to you.

Activity 1

MATERIALS:

☐ *Sort the "oo"* Activity Page (Appendix AM)
☐ Scissors
☐ Glue

DIRECTIONS:

1. Show your child the *Sort the "oo"* activity page.

2. Remind him that "oo" makes two different sounds. It makes a /u:/ (long "oo" sound, said "ew," like the word "room") and a // (short "oo" sound, said "uh," like the word "hook").

3. Ask him to cut out all of the words at the bottom of the activity page.

4. Ask your child to select a word and read it aloud.

5. He will then decide within which box to glue the word based on the "oo" sound. If it has a /u:/ (long "oo" sound like "moon") then he will glue the word in the first box. If it has a // (short "oo" sound like "book") then he will glue the word in the second box.

6. Continue until all words are glued in the appropriate box.

   Answer Key:

   1st box- zoo, soon, tool, bloom, pool, spoon

   2nd box- cook, foot, good, wood, food, took

● ● ●

Stories

Locate the Lesson 25 story titled "My Book." Fold the story into a book. Ask your child to read the story to you as many times as he would enjoy.

Optional comprehension questions to ask your child:

1. Where does the child like to read his book?

2. What kind of book do you think the child is reading? How do you know?

cut along line

hood

wood

good

stood

took

hook

book

cook

look

brook

shook

foot

fold

fold

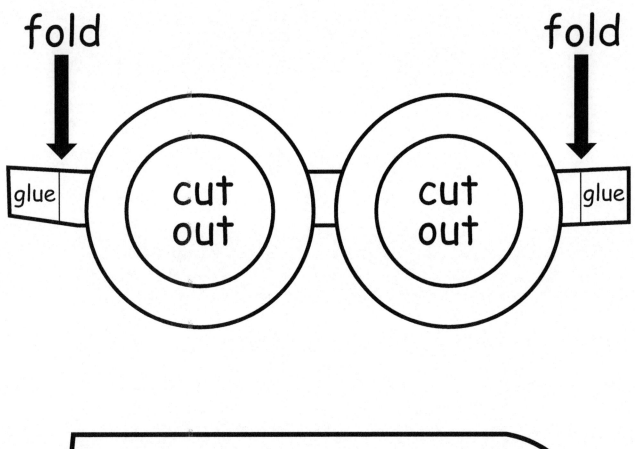

glue

cut
out

cut
out

glue

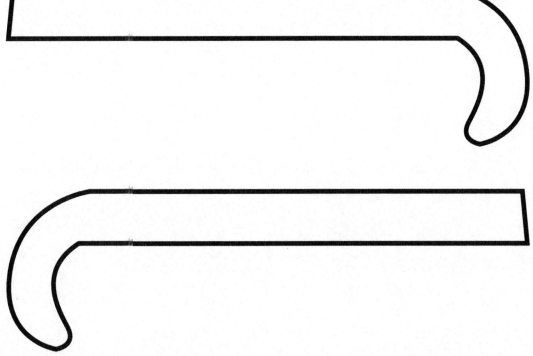

cut along line

OO like moon | OO like book

zoo	cook	soon	tool
foot	bloom	good	pool
wood	food	took	spoon

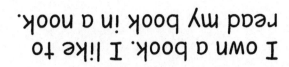

3

I learn to cook in my book.

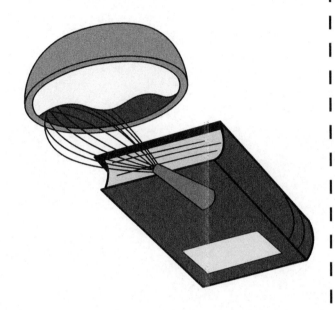

2

I own a book. I like to read my book in a nook.

It is a good book.

My Book

cut along line

{ New Words: who, from }

Activity 1

MATERIALS:

- ☐ *Memory Game* Activity Pages (Appendix AO)
- ☐ Scissors
- ☐ Colored Cardstock

DIRECTIONS:

1. Tell your child that he will learn two new sight words today. Sight words do not follow the rules for sounding out a word. So, you will tell him the word on the *Flashcards* for Lesson 26 and he will repeat the word. Practice the sight words several times.

2. Print the *Memory Game* activity pages on colored cardstock. This will help keep the words from being seen through the paper.

3. Cut out all of the cards on the activity pages and shuffle them.

4. Place the cards face down in four rows of seven cards.

5. Invite your child to play memory with you. Explain to him that he will choose any two cards and flip them over.

6. Next, he must read the sight words on the cards.

7. If the sight words do not match then he will flip them back over.

8. If the sight words match then he gets to keep the matching set and take another turn.

9. Now it will be your turn. You will follow the same rules in Steps 5-8.

10. The object of the game is to try to remember where sight words are hidden so matches can be located.

11. Continue playing until all matches have been found. The player with the most matches wins!

Stories

Locate the Lesson 26 story titled "The Note." Fold the story into a book. Ask your child to read the story to you as many times as he would enjoy.

You will notice the word "bookbag" in this story is highlighted green and orange. Explain to your child that this is a compound word (two words that combine to make one word). To help your child read compound words instruct him to read the green word first then the orange word and then he will combine the words to make one word.

Optional comprehension questions to ask your child:

1. What was in the child's bookbag?

2. What is written on the note?

3. Who is the note from?

who

from

cut along line

who

who

from

from

cut along line

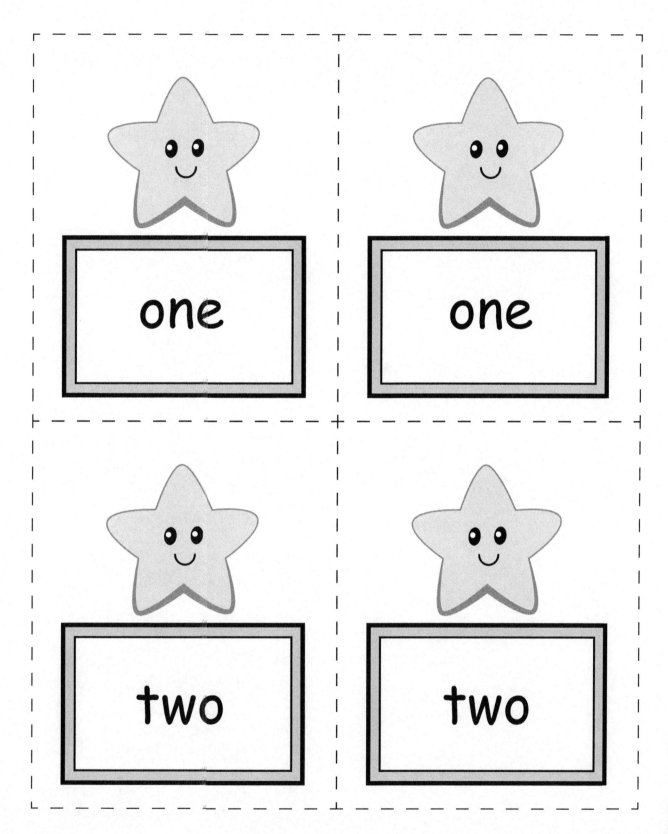

cut along line

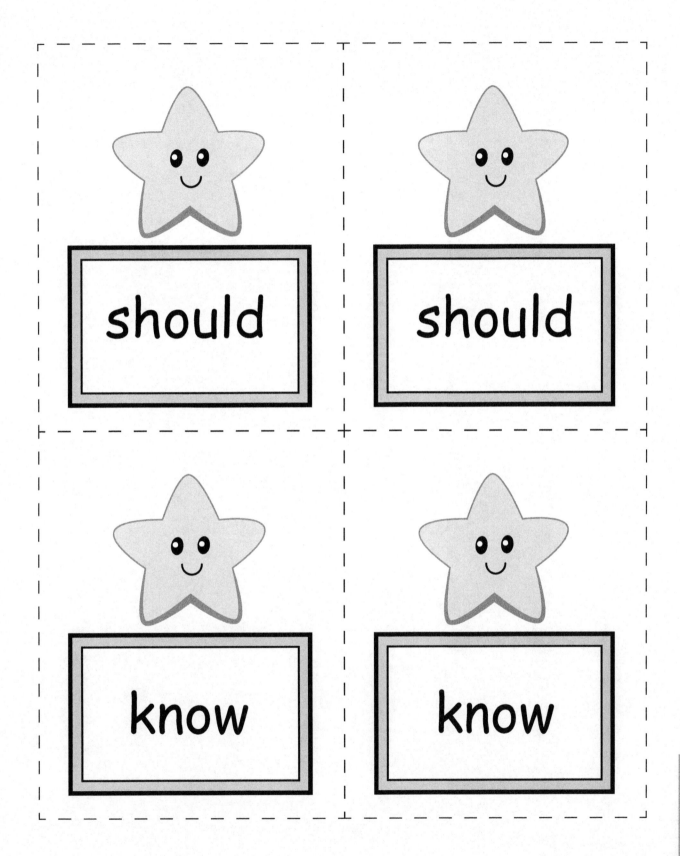

should

should

know

know

they

they

would

would

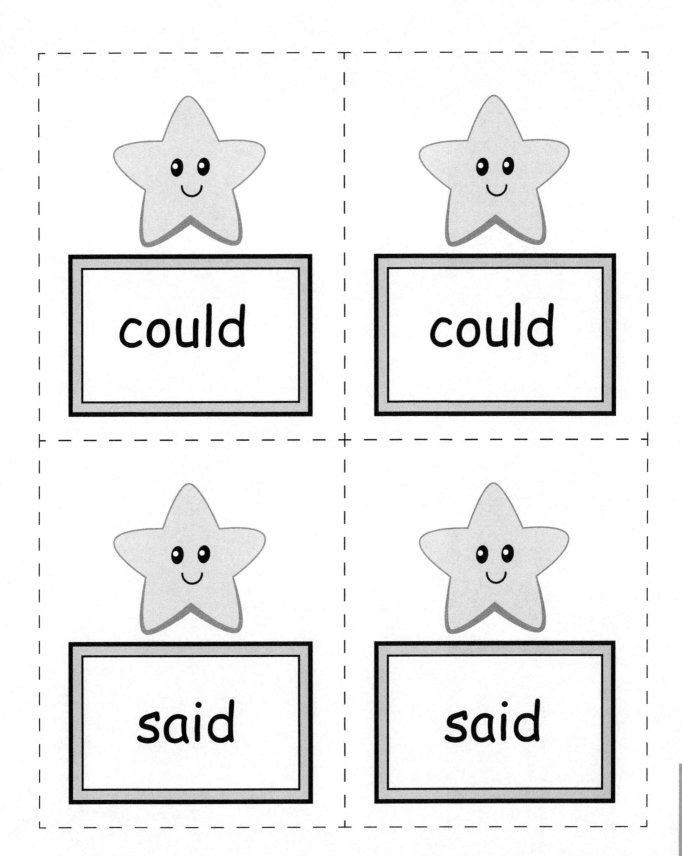

could

could

said

said

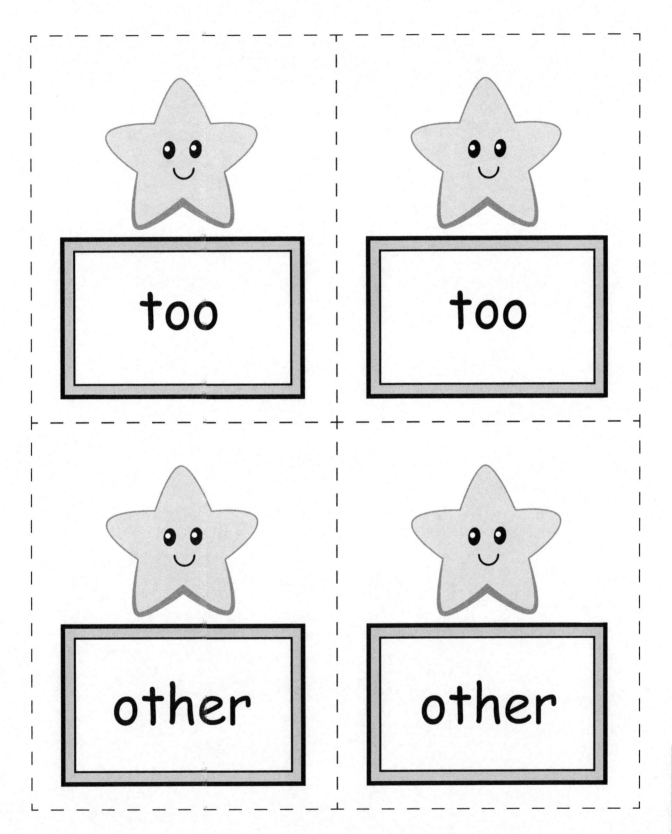

too

too

other

other

cut along line

cut along line

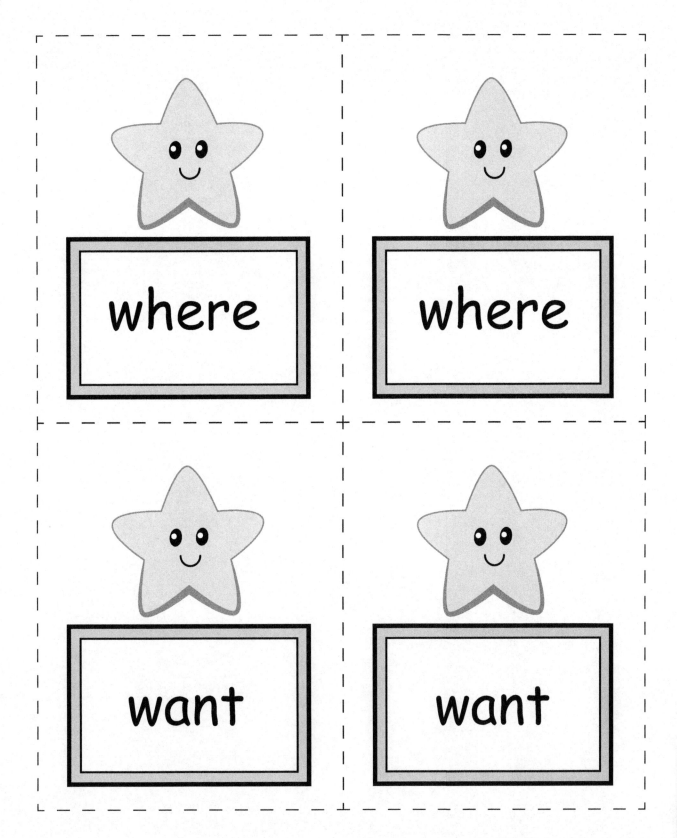

where

where

want

want

3

I look at the note. It has a blue star on it. Who is the note from?

2

I got a note in my bookbag. Who is the note from?

I soon know who the note is from. It is from my brother.

4

The Note

Lesson 26

1

{ **New Words: now, town, owl, power, flower, out, shout, hound, found, our, sour, mouth** }

Bonus Flashcards included in printable appendix:

how, cow, wow, down, gown, chow, howl, crowd, crown, tower, towel, frown, growl, shower, scout, sprout, sound, pound, round, ground, loud, hour, mount, cloud

Activity 1

MATERIALS:

☐ *"ow" and "ou" Pictures* Activity Page (Appendix AP)
☐ *Flashcards* for Lesson 27
☐ Highlighter

DIRECTIONS:

1. Tell your child that he will learn a sound today. The sound is "ow" like in the words "cow" and "mouse."

2. Show your child the "ow" and "ou" pictures on the activity page.

3. Point to the word "cow" on the activity page. Highlight the "ow" in the word. Tell your child that the "ow" says /ow/ like "ow, I'm hurt."

4. Now, point to the word "mouse" on the activity page. Highlight the "ou" in the word. Tell your child that the "ou" says /ow/ like "ow, I'm hurt" also. The "ou" is considered a diphthong because the two vowels blend together to make a new sound unlike either vowel sound.

5. Cut the activity page in half.

6. Place the cow picture on one end of the table and place the mouse picture on the other end of the table.

7. Explain to your child that you will hold up a *Flashcard* and he will read the word on the card.

8. After he reads the word, he will then sort the word by placing it on the correct picture. He will sort the word based on if it has an "ow" or "ou" that makes the /ow/ sound in the word.

   If the word has an "ou" in the word he just read, then he will place it on the mouse picture. If the word has an "ow" in the word he just read, then he will place it on the cow picture.

9. Continue playing until all words are sorted.

Activity 2

MATERIALS:

☐ Poster Board
☐ Markers
☐ Band-aids

DIRECTIONS:

1. On poster board, use markers to write as many New Words for Lesson 27 as can fit.

2. Show your child the poster board and band-aids. Ask him to tell you the sound he is currently learning, /ow/. Ask him what two groups of letters say that sound. ("ow" and "ou")

3. Explain to him that you will call out a word and he will need to locate the word on the poster board. Then he will place a band-aid on the word because the words say "ow."

4. Call out a word and wait as your child locates the word.

5. Once he locates it, ask him to read the word and then place a band-aid on the word.

6. Continue Steps 4 and 5 until all words are covered with a band-aid.

• • •

Stories

Locate the Lesson 27 story titled "Flowers.". Fold the story into a book. Ask your child to read the story to you as many times as he would enjoy.

Optional comprehension questions to ask your child:

1. In the book it says, "I like when flowers bloom." What do you think bloom means?

2. Have you ever made a flower crown?

3. What kind of flowers do you like?

now

town

owl

power

flower

out

shout

hound

found

our

sour

mouth

cow

mouse

3

I like to make flower crowns. I mount the crown on my head.

2

Flowers grow in the ground. I like when flowers bloom.

Flowers come in many colors like red, blue, and yellow. How I like flowers!

4

Lesson 27

Flowers

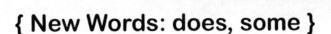

{ New Words: does, some }

Activity 1

MATERIALS:

☐ *Shape Writing* Activity Page (Appendix AQ)
☐ Pencil or Markers

DIRECTIONS:

1. Tell your child that he will learn two new sight words today. Sight words do not follow the rules for sounding out a word. So, you will tell him the word on the *Flashcards* for Lesson 28 and he will repeat the word. Practice the sight words a couple times.

2. Show your child the *Shape Writing* activity page.

3. Explain to him that he will write a sight word around the edge of each shape as many times as he can fit it.

4. Instruct him to look at the heart. Ask him to read the word on the edge of the heart, "does."

5. Now, ask him to trace the dotted letters of the word "does." He may trace the word with a pencil or it might be fun to use a marker.

6. Ask him to write the word "does" on the edge of the heart again and read the word.

7. Continue all the way around the heart until it is full. He can then count how many times he wrote the word "does" around the heart.

8. Continue Steps 4-7 with each shape.

● ● ●

Stories

Locate the Lesson 28 story titled "Clouds." Fold the story into a book. Ask your child to read the story to you as many times as he would enjoy.

Optional comprehension questions to ask your child:

1. What is the child looking at?

2. What shapes does the child see in the clouds?

3. Do you enjoy looking at the clouds?

Lesson 28

cut along line

does

some

cut along line

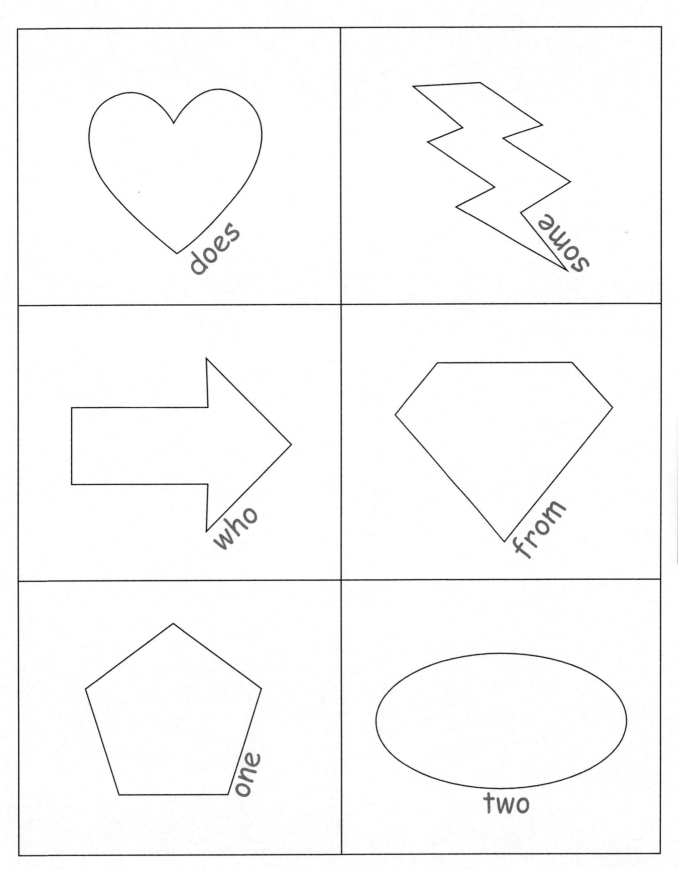

does

some

who

from

one

two

3

Does this cloud look like
a duck? Does this cloud
look like a cow?

2

Look at the clouds. Some
clouds look like art.

Lesson 28

Clouds

This cloud looks like a
boat.

4

Lesson 28

1

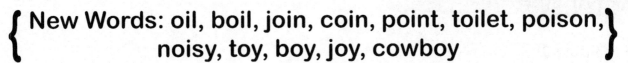
{ **New Words: oil, boil, join, coin, point, toilet, poison, noisy, toy, boy, joy, cowboy** }

Bonus Flashcards included in printable appendix:

soil, foil, spoil, joint, soy

Activity 1

MATERIALS:

- ☐ *Bump* Activity Page (Appendix AR)
- ☐ 2 Dice
- ☐ Counters

DIRECTIONS:

1. Tell your child that he will learn a sound today. The sound is /oi, oy/ like at the beginning of the word "oink." Explain that the letters "oi" and the letters "oy" make this new sound. This sound is another diphthong—two vowels that make a new sound.

2. Show your child an example of each kind of word on the *Flashcards* for Lesson 29. Allow him to practice reading the *Flashcards* for Lesson 29. Assist your child as needed.

3. Show your child the *Bump* activity page.

4. Give your child 12 counters of one color (coins, pom poms, goldfish, etc.). Set aside 12 counters of a different color for yourself as well.

5. Explain the rules to him. He will roll the two dice. Based on the number he rolled, he will place a counter on the mud puddle and read the word in the puddle.

6. If a player rolls a number that places his counter on a mud puddle that is occupied by another player's counter, the player "bumps" the opponent's counter off the mud puddle and places his own counter on the mud puddle. The counter (the one that was "bumped off" the mud puddle) is placed back into the opponent's "pile" of counters. The player whose counter is now located on the mud puddle should read the word on the mud puddle.

7. If a player rolls a number with his own counter on the mud puddle, then he can lock the mud puddle by placing a second counter on the mud puddle and reading the word. Now, when that number is rolled no one can go to that mud puddle.

8. Take turns rolling the dice and playing the game.

9. The first player to use all of his counters wins.

Lesson 29

Activity 2

MATERIALS:

☐ Bucket
☐ 5lb Bag of Rice
☐ *Flashcards*

DIRECTIONS:

1. Gather 15-20 *Flashcards* from Lessons 2-29. (Be intentional in your selection of *Flashcards*, selecting words which you believe would be most beneficial for your child to practice reading.)

2. Pour the rice into the bucket.

3. Fold each *Flashcard* in half.

4. Bury each *Flashcard* in the rice.

5. Ask your child to go for a hunt through the rice to uncover a word.

6. Once he locates a *Flashcard*, ask him to open it up and read the word.

7. Continue play until all words are located and read.

● ● ●

Stories

Locate the Lesson 29 story titled "The New Toy." Fold the story into a book. Ask your child to read the story to you as many times as he would enjoy.

Optional comprehension questions to ask your child:

1. What did the boy have to do to get a new toy?

2. How do you think he earned the money to get a new toy?

3. Do you think he is excited to buy his toy? How do you know?

oil

boil

join

coin

cut along line

point

toilet

poison

noisy

toy

boy

joy

cowboy

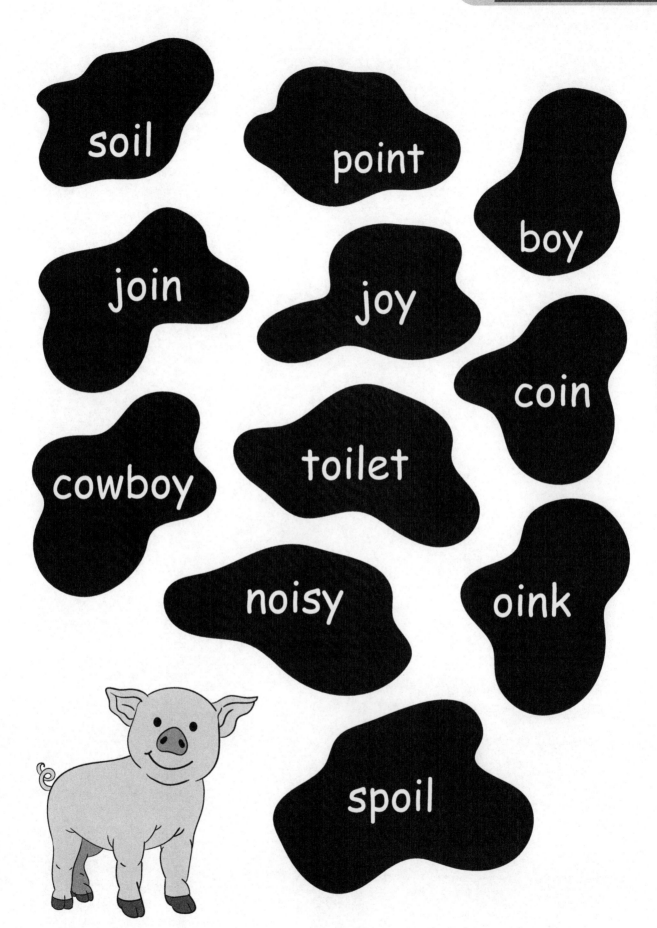

soil

point

boy

join

joy

coin

cowboy

toilet

noisy

oink

spoil

3

He and his dad go to the store. The boy points to the toy.

2

The boy jumps for joy. He has the coins to buy a new toy.

His dad hands the toy to the boy. The boy pays for the toy. The toy is now his toy!

4

The New Toy

Lesson 29

1

{ New Words: love, because }

Activity 1

MATERIALS:
- ☐ *Sight Word Graphing* Activity Page (Appendix AS)
- ☐ Markers or Colored Pencils

DIRECTIONS:

1. Tell your child that he will learn two new sight words today. Sight words do not follow the rules for sounding out a word. So, you will tell him the word on the *Flashcards* for Lesson 30 and he will repeat the word. Practice the sight words several times.

2. Show your child the *Sight Word Graphing* activity page.

3. Instruct your child to look at the graph at the bottom of the activity page. Ask him to read the words across the bottom of the graph to you.

4. Ask him to select a word from the graph. For example, the word "love."

5. Now, ask your child to look in the box at the top of the activity page to see how many times he can locate the word "love."

6. When he locates the word "love," ask your child to use a red marker or colored pencil to write the word in the column above "love," and then cross it out in the top box.

7. Repeat Steps 4-6 for the remaining words using the appropriate colors: because-orange, does-green, some-blue, who-purple, from-pink.

8. After the graph is complete, ask your child to determine which word has the most and least amounts.

• • •

Stories

Locate the Lesson 30 story titled "I Love You." Fold the story into a book. Ask your child to read the story to you as many times as he would enjoy.

Optional comprehension questions to ask your child:

1. What are the reasons the parent loves the child?

2. How does it make you feel when your parent tells you "I love you"?

love

because

3

I love you because you work hard.

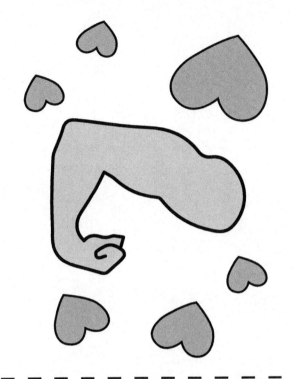

2

I love you because you are sweet.

I love you because you help me.

4

I Love You

Lesson 30

1

{ **New Words: haul, fault, August, pause, saw, law, jaw, straw, dawn, yawn, drawn, crawl** }

Bonus Flashcards included in printable appendix:

Paul, haunt, launch, fraud, paw, claw, draw, lawn, fawn

Activity 1

MATERIALS:

- ☐ *Cookie Snacks* Activity Pages (Appendix AT)
- ☐ Scissors
- ☐ 2 Paper Bags
- ☐ Glue
- ☐ Marker

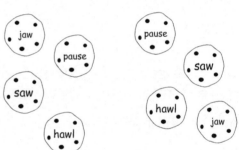

DIRECTIONS:

1. Tell your child that he will learn a new sound today. The sound is /ŏ/. The sound is similar to the sound a doctor might make when he says to his patient, "Open your mouth, stick out your tongue and say 'aww.'" Explain to your child that the letters "au" and the letters "aw" make this new sound.

2. Ask your child to help you cut out the cookies on the *Cookie Snacks* activity pages.

3. Cut out the picture of the boy and girl on the *Cookie Snacks* activity pages.

4. Ask your child to glue the boy onto the front of one paper bag. Then glue the girl onto the front of the other paper bag.

5. Cut out the mouth of both children so that there is a hole into each paper bag.

6. Label the girl bag with "au."

7. Label the boy bag with "aw."

8. Explain to your child that the children's mommy just made fresh cookies and the children want to try the delicious cookies. However, the little girl only likes cookies with "au" words and the little boy only likes cookies with "aw" words.

9. Ask him to pick up a cookie, read the word, and feed it to the correct child.

10. Continue playing until the children are full of cookies.

Activity 2

MATERIALS:

☐ *Read and Match* Activity Page (Appendix AU)
☐ Pencil

DIRECTIONS:

1. Show your child the *Read and Match* activity page.

2. Explain to him that he will read the word on the left-hand side of the activity page then locate the matching picture.

3. Once he locates the corresponding picture, he will draw a line from the word to the picture.

4. Continue until all eight words and pictures are matched.

• • •

Stories

Locate the Lesson 31 story titled "Drawing Contest.". Fold the story into a book. Ask your child to read the story to you as many times as he would enjoy.

Optional comprehension questions to ask your child:

1. What kind of contest did Paul enter?

2. What did he draw?

3. What picture would you draw for a drawing contest?

4. How do you think Paul feels when he wins?

haul

fault

August

pause

saw

law

jaw

straw

dawn

yawn

drawn

crawl

cut along line

cut along line

cut along line

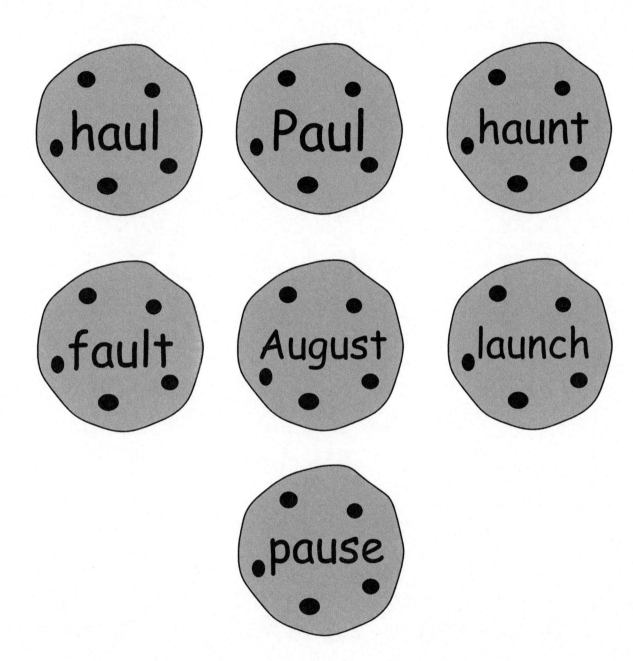

haul

Paul

haunt

fault

August

launch

pause

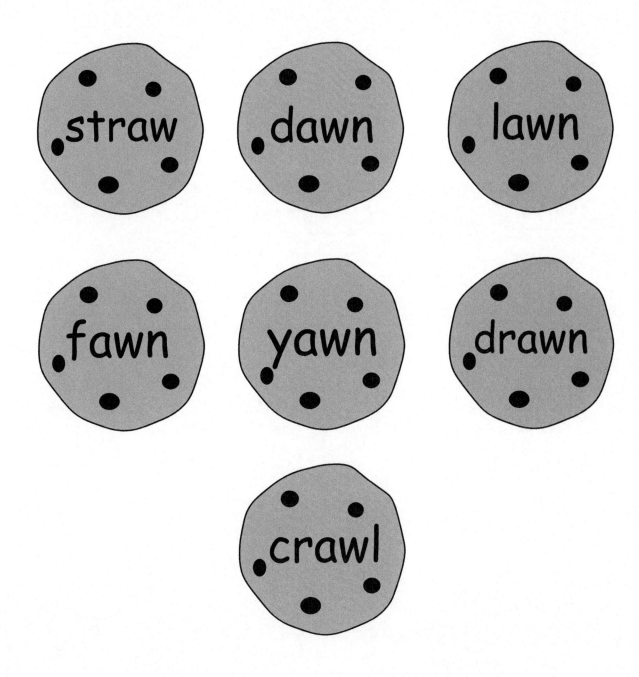

straw dawn lawn

fawn yawn drawn

crawl

cut along line

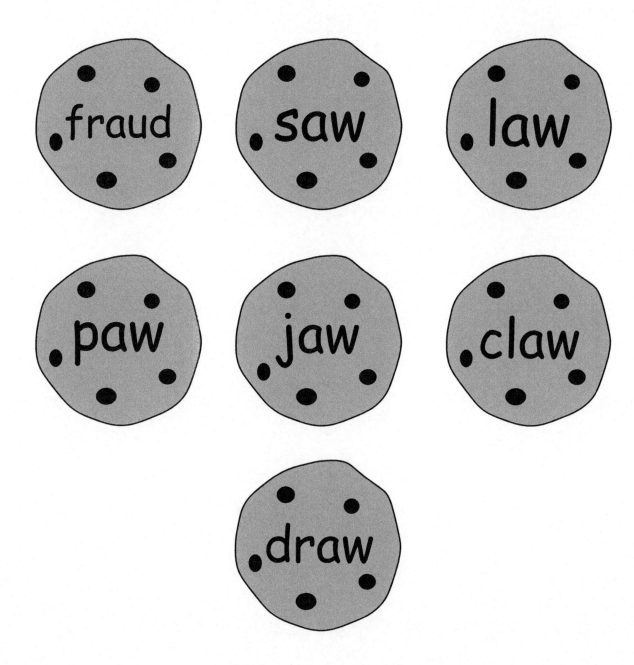

straw

crawl

coin

cowboy

frown

cloud

moon

lawn

3

Paul draws a brown fawn in the lawn.

2

Paul saw a sign for a drawing contest. Paul enters the contest in August.

DRAWING CONTEST THIS AUGUST

Drawing Contest

Paul's drawing comes in first place. He won!

4

Lesson 31

1

Lesson 31

{**New Words: all, tall, fall, small, call, talk, salt, palm, metal, album, pedal, chalk**}

Bonus Flashcards included in printable appendix:

wall, ball, walk, calm, bald, medal

Activity 1

MATERIALS:

- ☐ 18 Craft Foam Shapes
- ☐ Sharpie
- ☐ Tupperware Container
- ☐ Shaving Cream
- ☐ Cup of Water

DIRECTIONS:

1. Prepare the activity by writing one New Word (all, tall, wall, ball, fall, small, call, talk, walk, salt, palm, calm, bald, metal, album, medal, pedal, chalk) on each craft foam shape with a Sharpie marker.

2. Tell your child that he will learn a sound today. The sound is /al/ like in the word "tall." Explain that the letters "al" make this new sound.

3. Fill a Tupperware container with shaving cream. (This activity gets messy so it is a good idea to do this activity outside.)

4. Insert the foam shapes into the shaving cream.

5. Explain to your child that he will hunt through the shaving cream to find 18 treasures.

6. Once he finds a treasure, he can dip it into the cup of water to clean the shaving cream off.

7. Next, ask your child to read the word on the foam shape.

8. Continue hunting for treasure until all 18 words are located and read.

Stories

Locate the Lesson 32 story titled "The Tall Boy." Fold the story into a book. Ask your child to read the story to you as many times as he would enjoy.

On page 3, your child will read the word "learned." To read this word it might be helpful to cover up the "ed" and ask your child to sound out "learn." Explain to him that the "ed" at the end of the word makes a /d/ sound. So, the word is "learned." The "ed" at the end of words show that the action happened in the past.

Optional comprehension questions to ask your child:

1. Why do you think it was hard for the tall boy to walk?

2. How did the boy learn not to fall?

3. What does the boy become good at?

all

tall

fall

small

call

talk

salt

palm

metal

album

pedal

chalk

1

The Tall Boy

Soon the boy was very good at ball. His mother and father cheer for him.

4

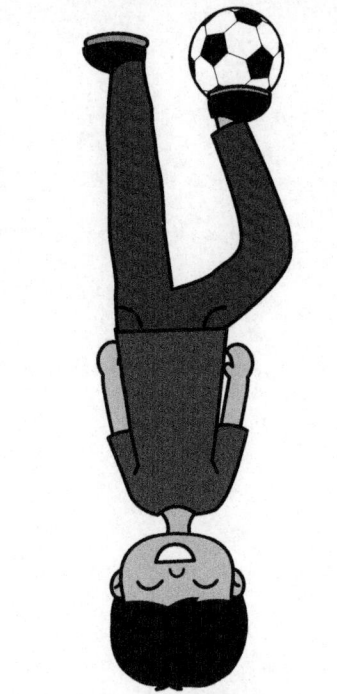

There was a boy who was not small. He was tall.

2

It was hard to walk because he was tall. But he learned not to fall.

3

{ New Words: been, whose, about }

Activity 1

MATERIALS:

- ☐ *Say It, Make It, Write It* Activity Page (Appendix AV)
- ☐ *Flashcards* for Lesson 33
- ☐ Page Protector
- ☐ Wooden or Magnetic Letters
- ☐ Dry Erase Marker

DIRECTIONS:

1. Tell your child that he will learn three new sight words today. Sight words do not follow the rules for sounding out a word. So, you will tell him the word on the *Flashcards* for Lesson 33 and he will repeat the word. Practice the sight words several times.

2. Show your child the *Say It, Make It, Write It* activity page. Insert the activity page into a page protector.

3. Place one of the new sight word *Flashcards* for Lesson 33 in the "Say It" box.

4. Ask your child to say the word.

5. Now, he will use the wooden or magnetic letters to build the sight word in the "Make It" box. Ask him to read the word to you.

6. Lastly, he will use a dry erase marker to write the sight word in the "Write It" box. Ask him to read the word again.

7. Repeat Steps 3-6 with the other two sight words for Lesson 33. This is a great activity to continue practicing sight words from previous lessons, or words that your child needs a little extra practice with.

Lesson 33

Stories

Locate the Lesson 33 story titled "Bear." Fold the story into a book. Ask your child to read the story to you as many times as he would enjoy.

On page 4, your child will read the word "started." To read this word it might be helpful to cover up the "ed" and allow your child to sound out "start." Remind your child that the "ed" at the end of the word makes a /d/ sound. So, the word is "started." The "ed" at the end of words show that the action happened in the past.

Optional comprehension questions to ask your child:

1. Was the bear nice at the beginning of the story? How do you know?

2. What did the mouse do? Was that nice?

3. What do you think made bear start to be nice?

been

whose

about

cut along line

Say It

Make It

Write It

_____

– – – – – – – – – –

_____

cut along line

3

The mouse gave bear his own toy. The bear felt happy.

2

There was a bear whose toy was not to share. The bear said, "Who has been playing with my toy?"

Lesson 33

Bear

Lesson 33

1

The bear was no longer mean. The bear started to share.

4

{ **New Words: cent, center, cell, city, acid, fancy, mercy, pencil, face, race, lace, nice** }

Bonus Flashcards included in printable appendix:

mice, rice, price, spice, slice

Activity 1

MATERIALS:

☐ *Cut and Sort* Activity Page (Appendix AW)
☐ Scissors
☐ Glue

DIRECTIONS:

1. Tell your child that he will learn a new sound today. The sound is /s/, but it is made by the letter "c" as in the word "city." This is called a soft "c" sound. A "c" is soft when an "e, i, y" comes after the "c."

2. Show your child the *Cut and Sort* activity page.

3. Explain to your child that some of the words have a hard "c" and say /c/, but some of the words have soft "c" and say /s/. He will need to cut out each picture.

4. Next, ask your child if the picture or word has a soft or hard "c" sound.

5. Once he decides what sound the "c" makes he will glue it in the appropriate box.

6. Continue until all pictures are glued in the correct location.

   Answer Key:

   Soft "c"-city, cent, cereal, celery

   Hard "c"-cat, cloud, cake, crown

Activity 2

MATERIALS:

☐ *Write and Sort* Activity Page (Appendix AX)
☐ Pencil

DIRECTIONS:

1. Your child will continue to practice sorting the soft and hard "c" sound to reinforce what he has learned.

2. Show your child the *Write and Sort* activity page.

3. Ask your child to look at the word bank box at the bottom of the activity page and read the first word in the box, "price."

4. Ask your child if the word has a soft or hard "c." If it has a soft "c" sound he will write the word in the soft "c" column. However, if it has a hard "c" sound he will write the word in the hard "c" column. The word "price" has a soft "c," so it will be written in the soft "c" column.

5. Repeat Steps 3 and 4 until all words are sorted.

   Answer Key:

   Soft "c" Words-price, mice, race, cent, center, cell

   Hard "c" Words-coat, cart, cow, coin, claw, scream

● ● ●

Stories

Locate the Lesson 34 story titled "Dinner." Fold the story into a book. Ask your child to read the story to you as many times as he would enjoy.

Optional comprehension questions to ask your child:

1. Where did the mice go for dinner?

2. What did the mice have for dinner?

3. What is your favorite dinner to eat?

cut along line

cent

center

cell

city

cut along line

acid

fancy

mercy

pencil

face

race

lace

nice

Hard c /k/	Soft c /k/

Soft c (s)	Hard c (k)
_____	_____
- - - - - - -	- - - - - - -
_____	_____
_____	_____
- - - - - - -	- - - - - - -
_____	_____
- - - - - - -	- - - - - - -
_____	_____
- - - - - - -	- - - - - - -
_____	_____
- - - - - - -	- - - - - - -
_____	_____
- - - - - - -	- - - - - - -
_____	_____

price   coat   mice   cart   race   cow

cent   center   coin   claw   cell   scream

3

The other mouse asked for cheese with spice.

One mouse picked rice. The other mouse asked for cheese with spice.

The mice sat down. One mouse picked rice. The other mouse asked for cheese with spice.

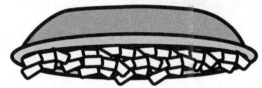

2

They made plans for a fancy dinner.

Two mice went to the city. They made plans for a fancy dinner.

Dinner

After dinner the mice split a pie.

cut along line

{ **New Words: germ, gem, digit, age, cage, charge, change, huge, large, gerbil, engine, judge** }

Bonus Flashcards included in printable appendix:

gel, bridge, orange. stage

Activity 1

MATERIALS:

☐ *Gorilla and Giraffe Flipbook* Activity Pages (Appendix AY)
☐ Scissors
☐ Glue
☐ Crayons

DIRECTIONS:

1. Tell your child that he will learn a new sound today. The sound is /j/, but it is made by the letter "g" like in the word "germ." This is called a soft "g" sound. A "g" is soft when an "e, i, y" comes after the "g."

2. Show your child page 1 and 3 of the *Gorilla and Giraffe Flipbook* activity pages.

3. Ask him to identify the gorilla. Ask him to identify the beginning sound of "gorilla." It is a hard "g" sound.

4. Ask your child to identify the giraffe. Ask him to identify the beginning sound of "giraffe." It sounds like a "j," but it is a "g." It is a soft "g."

5. Your child may color the gorilla and giraffe.

6. Cut out the animal shapes on each activity page.

7. Fold the gorilla and giraffe head upward along the dotted line.

8. Use a glue stick to rub glue along the top portion of the gorilla shaped head with pictures (page 2).

9. Place the colored gorilla head on top of the gorilla shaped head with pictures. Your child should be able to lift the gorilla's mouth and see pictures that begin with a hard "g."

10. Ask your child to read the hard "g" words on the gorilla's mouth.

10. Now use a glue stick to rub glue along the top portion of the giraffe shaped head with pictures (page 4).

11. Place the colored giraffe head on top of the giraffe shaped head with pictures. Your child should be able to lift the giraffe's mouth and see pictures with a soft "g" sound.

12. Ask your child to sound out the soft "g" words and read them.

• • •

Activity 2

MATERIALS:

☐ *Soft "g" Reading* Activity Pages (Appendix AZ)
☐ Yellow and Green Marker

DIRECTIONS:

1. Show your child the *Soft "g" Reading* activity page.

2. Explain to him that he will read the story through one time without doing anything.

3. Next, he will go back and read it again. When he comes across a word in the story with a "g" he will determine if the "g" has a hard "g" (/g/) or soft "g" (/j/) sound.

4. If the "g" has a /j/ sound, then he will highlight the "g" with a yellow marker.

5. If the "g" has a /g/ sound, then he will highlight the "g" with a green marker.

   Answer Key:

   Yellow Highlighted Words: George, bridge, cage, orange, George, giraffe, giraffe, huge, giraffe, age, George, George

   Green Highlighted Words: gorillas, long, get, gorilla, got, gorillas, gorilla, eating, goodbye

6. Encourage your child to read the story through again after he has highlighted the "g's." This will help build fluency.

Stories

Locate the Lesson 35 story titled "The Bunny." Fold the story into a book. Ask your child to read the story to you as many times as he would enjoy.

Optional comprehension questions to ask your child:

1. What did Brett see in the field?

2. What does Brett want to do with the bunny?

3. What do you think you need to do to care for a bunny?

cut along line

germ

gem

digit

age

cage

charge

change

huge

large

gerbil

engine

judge

Hard g

cut along line

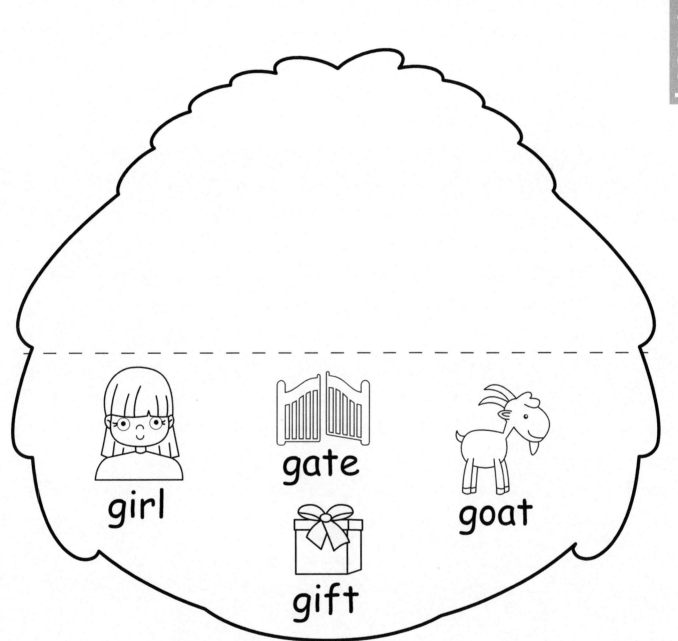

girl

gate

gift

goat

cut along line

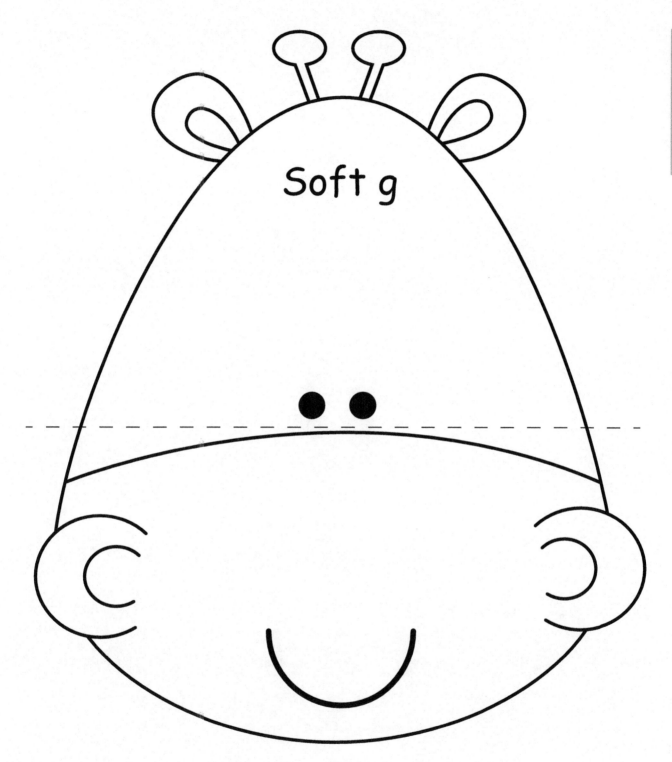

Soft g

cut along line

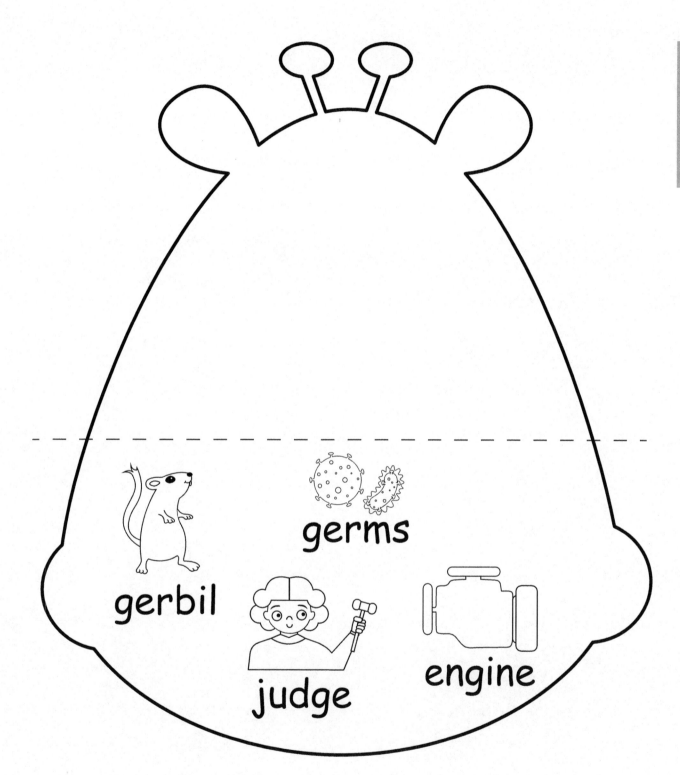

gerbil

germs

judge

engine

■ = Soft "g" (j)

■ = Hard "g" (g)

Read the story. As you read, highlight all soft "g" sounds with yellow. Highlight all hard "g" sounds with green.

George went to the zoo. He wanted to see the gorillas. He crossed a long bridge to get to the gorilla cage. When he got to the gorillas, he saw a young gorilla eating an orange. Next, George went to see a giraffe. The giraffe was huge! The zoo keeper said there was a giraffe that was seven years old. That is the same age as George. George said goodbye to the animals as he left the zoo.

Lesson 35

3

Brett wants to make the bunny his pet. He gets a huge cage to catch the bunny.

2

Brett saw a large bunny hopping in the field.

Brett knows he will have to change the bunny's cage.

The Bunny

{ **New Words: phone, phase, graph, phrase, dolphin, elephant** }

Activity 1

MATERIALS:

☐ *Complete the Sentence* Activity Page (Appendix BA)
☐ Pencil

DIRECTIONS:

1. Tell your child that he will learn a new sound today. The sound is /f/, but it is made by the letters "ph" like in the word "phone."

2. Ask your child to practice reading the *Flashcards* for Lesson 36.

3. Show your child the *Complete the Sentence* activity page.

4. Instruct him to read the sentence and choose the best word from the boxes below each sentence that completes the sentence.

5. Ask your child to circle the correct word in the box.

   Answer Key:

   1. Phone

   2. Dolphin

   3. Elephant

Activity 2

MATERIALS:

☐ *Which Sound?* Activity Page (Appendix BB)
☐ Pencil

DIRECTIONS:

1. In this activity your child will practice identifying the "ph" sound using the *Which Sound?* Activity page.

2. Show your child the activity page.

3. Ask your child to tell you the name of the first picture. (It is a picture of a "graph.")

4. Ask him if he hears a "ph" sound, /f/, or "sh" sound, /sh/.

5. Once he determines the sound he hears in the word, ask him to circle the correct sound.

6. Continue Steps 3-5 for the remaining pictures on the activity page.

   Answer Key:
   1. ph
   2. ch
   3. th
   4. ph
   5. sh
   6. ph
   7. wh
   8. ph

* * *

Stories

Locate the Lesson 36 story titled "The Phone Call." Fold the story into a book. Ask your child to read the story to you as many times as he would enjoy.

Optional comprehension questions to ask your child:

1. Who is sad?

2. Who does Elephant call?

3. Who makes you happy to receive a phone call from?

cut along line

phone

phase

graph

phrase

dolphin

elephant

Gabby talks to her mom on the _____.

phone	pony

The _____ makes a big splash.

donkey	dolphin

The _____ cools off in the river.

llama	elephant

ph

wh

th

sh

sh

ch

ph

ch

th

ph

wh

sh

sh

ph

sh

ph

3

Dolphin is happy to get a phone call.

2

Elephant is sad. Elephant will make a phone call to dolphin.

Elephant talks to dolphin.
She starts to feel happy!

4

The Phone Call

Lesson 36

Lesson 36

{ **New Words: write, wrist, wrench, wreath, gnat, gnaw, gnash, knee, knit, knife, knot, knew** }

Bonus Flashcards included in printable appendix:

wrote, wrap, wrong, wreck, sign, knock, knight

Activity 1

MATERIALS:

☐ *Ghost Letters* Activity Page (Appendix BC)
☐ 3 White Paper Lunch Bags
☐ Glue or Tape
☐ Scissors
☐ *Flashcards* for Lesson 37

DIRECTIONS:

1. Instruct your child that some letters are silent and don't make a sound in the word. These are called ghost letters. In the digraph "wr" the "w" is silent—the digraph makes the sound /r/. In the digraph "gn" the "g" is silent—the digraph makes the sound /n/. In the digraph "kn" the "k" is silent—the digraph makes the sound /n/.

2. Cut out the ghosts on the *Ghost Letters* activity page.

3. Glue one ghost on the front of each of the three white paper lunch bags.

4. Show your child each ghost and review the sounds of the digraphs.

5. Present your child with the *Flashcards* for Lesson 37.

6. Explain to him that he will read the word on the *Flashcard* and then sort it into the corresponding ghost letter bag. You might have to remind him of the silent letters as he begins this activity.

7. Once the *Flashcards* are sorted, empty each bag and ask him to read the words from the bag again to make sure he sorted them correctly.

Lesson 37

Activity 2

MATERIALS:

☐ *Drawing Ghosts* Activity Page (Appendix BD)
☐ Crayon

DIRECTIONS:

1. Tell your child that in this activity he will practice identifying more ghost letters.

2. Show your child the *Drawing Ghosts* activity page.

3. Explain to him that he will read the word in each box. If the word has a ghost letter or silent letter, then he will draw a ghost around the silent letter.

4. Tell your child that not every word on the activity page will have a ghost letter.

5. Ask your child to look at the first word, "write" and read the word.

6. Direct your child's attention to the outline of a ghost around the "w." (As noted, this signifies the "w" is silent.) Ask him to trace the ghost.

7. Continue until the activity page is complete.

    Answer Key:

    <u>W</u>rite

    <u>W</u>rap

    <u>G</u>nat

    <u>K</u>nit

    <u>K</u>nife

    <u>W</u>rong

    <u>K</u>new

    <u>G</u>naw

    <u>K</u>nock

Stories

Locate the Lesson 37 story titled "The Knight." Fold the story into a book. Ask your child to read the story to you as many times as he would enjoy.

Optional comprehension questions to ask your child:

1. What was the knight taking to the princess?

2. How was he going to deliver the note?

3. What do you think the note says?

4. Do you think the knight will be able to deliver the note to the princess?

write

wrist

wrench

wreath

gnat

gnaw

gnash

knee

knit

knife

knot

knew

write	wrap
germ	gnat
knit	knife
wrong	knew
gnaw	wash
kick	knock

cut along line

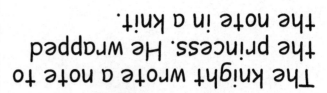

3

The knight went to get his horse. His horse was gnawing on a carrot. He got up on his horse.

2

The knight wrote a note to the princess. He wrapped the note in a knit.

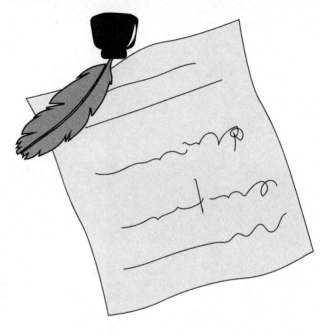

The knight went to take the note to the princess. He went the wrong way. He must go the other way.

4

The Knight

Lesson 37

1

Lesson 37

Reading fluency is the ability to read accurately, smoothly, and with expression. Fluent readers are able to recognize words without decoding. Fluency is an important part in the learning to read process. It allows a child to bridge the gap between word recognition to reading comprehension. Fluency allows children to focus on what the text is saying instead of concentrating on decoding words. This is a skill, just like learning to read, that comes with practice and through good modeling.

Continue to read aloud to your child. The best way to demonstrate fluency is through modeling. Model what a good reader does—show your child how to pause after punctuation, change your tone for exclamation or questions, or even change your voice for characters.

I have included some fun activities below to help your child practice his new reading skills and work his way to becoming a fluent reader.

Activity 1

MATERIALS:

- ☐ 12 *Flashcards*
- ☐ Dry Erase Marker
- ☐ Dry Erase Board

DIRECTIONS:

1. Select 12 *Flashcards* from any of the 37 Lessons. I recommend choosing words that are challenging to your child to help him practice word recognition.

2. Choose one of the *Flashcards* and ask your child to write the word onto his dry erase board. If you do not have a dry erase board, please use a window or white sheet of paper inside a page protector.

3. Explain to your child that each sentence ends with a punctuation mark—period (.), exclamation point (!), or question mark (?). Explain to him that a sentence that ends with a period is telling a statement or command and is read with an even toned voice. A sentence that ends with an exclamation point emphasizes what is being said and may be indicative of strong emotions regarding the words which have been written. They may be words of joy, anger, or excitement. The words preceding the exclamation mark are typically read with a strong and forceful/excited tone. A sentence that ends in a question mark asks a question and is read with a slight inflection in your voice at the end of the sentence.

4. Show your child some examples of each sentence.

5. After he has written the word onto the dry erase board ask him to add a punctuation mark at the end of the word. You may assign the word a period (.), exclamation point (!), or question mark (?).

6. Now, ask him to practice reading the word with the punctuation mark in the correct tone.

7. Practice three times before trying Steps 2-6 with the remaining 11 *Flashcards*.

Lesson 38

Activity 2

MATERIALS:

☐ *Punctuation Practice* Activity Page (Appendix BE)
☐ Scissors

DIRECTIONS:

1. Show your child the *Punctuation Practice* activity page.

2. Ask him to cut out the punctuation marks at the bottom of the activity page.

3. Ask him to place one punctuation mark at the end of each sentence—any punctuation mark he chooses.

4. Ask your child to look at the first sentence and tell you the punctuation mark that is at the end of the sentence.

5. Ask him how he will read the sentence based on the punctuation mark. (He will read with a regular voice if it ends with a period, an excited voice if it ends with an exclamation point, and he will raise his voice at the end of the sentence if it ends with a question mark.)

6. Now, ask your child to read the first sentence with the correct tone and voice.

7. Repeat Steps 4-6 for the second and third sentence.

8. After your child has read each sentence, ask him to move the punctuation marks around so each sentence has a new punctuation mark.

9. Repeat the same process to practice reading the sentences with differing punctuation marks.

● ● ●

Activity 3

MATERIALS:

☐ *Reading Tree* Activity Page (Appendix BF)
☐ Pencil
☐ Crayons

DIRECTIONS:

1. Show your child the *Reading Tree* activity page.

2. Explain to him that he will read each line on the activity page by placing his finger on the star under the word to read the word. Each line adds one more word to the sentence.

3. After he reads the complete sentence, he will repeat the reading tree three times.

4. Now, ask your child to answer the questions at the bottom of the activity page. Help him read the questions or instructions as needed.

The Ultimate Teach Your Child to Read Activity Book: Developing Reader Autumn McKay

Activity 4

MATERIALS:

☐ *Scooping Phrases* Activity Pages (Appendix BG)
☐ Markers
☐ White Board
☐ Dry Erase Markers
☐ Scissors

DIRECTIONS:

1. In this lesson you will begin to teach your child how to scoop phrases instead of pointing to each individual word of a sentence. This will help the sentences sound smoother and help your child begin to understand the sentences meaning.

2. Write this sentence on a white board: "I like to look at the bright moon from my window."

3. Read the sentence you wrote out loud to your child by placing your finger under each word you read. Your reading of the sentence should sound like a robot speaking.

4. Ask your child if he would enjoy if you read books in this manner.

5. Explain to him that when you read books you scoop phrases together so that it sounds smooth and is easier to understand.

6. Show him how you would scoop the sentence on the white board. Take a different colored dry erase marker and draw a line under the phrases (each phrase can be a different color) you read together. For example, I would scoop the following phrases, "<u>I like to look at</u> <u>the bright moon</u> <u>from my window</u>." But your phrases might be different.

7. Now, read the scooped phrases to your child by sliding your finger under the phrases instead of each word. So, it would be read, "I like to look at...the bright moon...from my window," with a slight pause in between each phrase.

8. Show your child the *Scooping Phrases* activity pages.

9. There are four sets of reading cards. Each set has three boxes with the same sentence. Please cut apart the four sets.

10. Show your child the first set of reading cards. For example, "The muffin is in the basket."

11. Ask him to look at Box 1 and place his finger under each word as he reads the sentence.

12. Now, ask your child to look at Box 2. The sentence has been broken apart into phrases. He will now read the phrases of the sentence by sliding his finger along the curved line of the phrase instead of pointing at each word.

13. In Box 3, he will be allowed to draw his own scooped phrases with a marker. Then he will look at the face in front of the sentence to see with which emotion to read the scooped sentence he created.

14. Repeat Steps 9-13 for the other three sets of reading cards.

Activity 5

MATERIALS:

☐ Stories From Previous Lessons

DIRECTIONS:

1. Your child will practice reading like he talks. Ask him to choose a story from a previous Lesson.

2. Ask him to read the story through one time. In his first reading of the story, it might sound choppy or as if he is reading the story in slow motion, word by word.

3. If he would like, he may scoop phrases in each sentence and read the story for a second time. This time it will sound smoother.

4. Take a brief break.

5. Come back to the story and ask your child to read it another time. The more he practices reading the same story, the easier it is for his brain to remember the words he is reading and to be able to recall the words for a faster, smoother reading.

6. I recommend doing this activity a couple times throughout the week with different stories.

● ● ●

Activity 6

MATERIALS:

☐ Stories From Previous Lessons

DIRECTIONS:

1. Please select a story from a previous Lesson. (You may also choose a book from your home or library that your child is able to read.) This activity is called echo reading, because after you demonstrate to your child how to read fluently with pacing and inflection, your child mimics your example.

2. Read the first page of the story by scooping phrases, demonstrating the correct vocal tones for punctuation, and even adding character voices if there is a person talking.

3. Now, ask your child to read the first page in the same manner you read the first page.

4. Continue Steps 2 and 3 until the book is complete.

Activity 7

MATERIALS:

- ☐ *Fluency Self Check* Activity Page (Appendix BH)
- ☐ Stories From Previous Lessons
- ☐ Recording Device

DIRECTIONS:

1. Please choose a story from a previous Lesson. (You may also pick a book from your home or library that your child is able to read.)

2. If you have a smart phone, download a free voice recorder app, or utilize some other recording device.

3. Ask your child to read the selected story. Tell your child you will be recording him as he reads the story so he will be able to hear how he reads. (Your child may want to practice reading the story several times before feeling comfortable being recorded.) If your child struggles with some of the words, assist him as needed. Do not record your child until your child is confident in the pronunciation of the words being read. Discard any recording you feel might be embarrassing to your child and record again. This should be fun.

4. Once the recording is complete, hand him the *Fluency Self Check* activity page. Explain to him that he will be listening to his reading to determine what kind of reader he was in the reading of the selected story.

   Review with your child the questions on the *Fluency Self Check*. Explain to your child that as he listens to the recording you would like him to answer the following questions.

   Discuss with your child the first question on the activity page. Ask your child to listen for the phrase that is best descriptive of the manner he read the story. Did he read like a robot in a very choppy voice pausing after each word? Did he read like a roller coaster where he read so fast that all of the words blended together to sound like one word? Did he read like he talks on the phone to a family member? As he listens to his recording, ask your child to circle the statement that best describes how he read the story.

   Point to the second question on the activity page. Ask your child to listen for the manner he vocally expressed himself in tone and volume when reading the story. Remind your child how the voice should change with the different punctuations or characters speaking. If he read the story without appropriate expression he will mark a sad face, a straight face if he does a little, and a happy face if he read the story with expression throughout the book.

   Point to the last question on the activity page. Instruct your child that when he listens to the recording you want him to determine if his reading sounded as if he read the story scooping phrases together or word by word. Tell your child that if he thinks he read the story word by word then he will mark the sad face, if he scooped a few phrases he can mark the straight face, and if he read the whole book by scooping phrases then he can mark a happy face.

5. Play the recording and allow him time to determine how he read the selected story.

6. After he has marked his *Fluency Self Check* page, discuss with your child his thoughts and ways he can continue to work on becoming a more fluent reader.

7. I recommend saving the recording and doing this activity once or twice a week so your child can listen to his progress as he becomes a more fluent reader.

Activity 8

MATERIALS:

- ☐ *Reading Race* Activity Page (Appendix B1)
- ☐ 2 Dry Erase Markers
- ☐ 2 Page Protectors
- ☐ Stopwatch

DIRECTIONS:

1. Show your child the *Reading Race* activity page. It is a story titled *Our Beach Trip*.

2. Print out two copies of the *Reading Race* activity page.

3. Place each activity page in a page protector.

4. Explain to him that he will be racing against himself in this activity.

5. Tell your child that he will have two minutes to read out loud as much of the story as he can within that time. As he is reading, he needs to concentrate on punctuation, inflection in his voice, and scoop phrasing.

6. Ask your child to tell you when he is ready to begin.

7. Start the timer and say "Go."

8. Listen to him as he is reading, quietly mark any words he reads incorrectly on your *Reading Race* activity page with a dry erase marker.

9. When the two-minute timer ends, ask your child to circle the last word he read on his activity page.

10. Review any of the words you have marked on your activity page with your child so he can work on correcting those mistakes.

11. Erase your activity page, but allow him to keep the circled word on his activity page.

12. Reset the timer, and get your child ready to read for round two of the reading race.

13. As you did previously, mark any words he reads incorrectly on your activity page.

14. Repeat Steps 9-11.

15. Repeat Steps 6-11 for round three of the reading race.

16. Congratulate your child if he increased the number of words read in each round. If he did not increase the numbers of words read, find something to encourage him about. For example, you could commend your child for correctly reading a word he mispronounced the first time, reading with inflection, scooping phrases, etc.

17. This is also a good activity to do with books. Just use a pencil to mark the words so that you can erase the marks.

Activity 9

MATERIALS:

☐ Stories From Previous Lessons

DIRECTIONS:

1. Please pick a story from a previous Lesson. (You may also select a book from your home or library that your child is able to read.)

2. For this activity, you will assign your child an emotion for which to read the story. For example, the assigned emotion could be happy, sad, mad, surprised, tired, etc.

3. Allow your child to read the story in the assigned emotion by changing his voice to match the emotion.

4. Assign another emotion and ask him to read the story again.

5. Allow him to read the story in at least three different emotions.

● ● ●

Activity 10

MATERIALS:

☐ Stories From Previous Lessons

DIRECTIONS:

1. Please pick a story from a previous Lesson. (You may also choose a book from your home or library that your child is able to read.) You will need two copies of the story or book.

2. Hand your child a copy of the story and you will use the other copy.

3. Sit side by side with your child.

4. Ask him to follow along in his book as you read from your book. You may use your finger to slide underneath the words of the story and ask him to do the same thing.

5. Slowly, but smoothly read the story.

Lesson 38

Activity 11

MATERIALS:

- ☐ Stories From Previous Lessons
- ☐ Pet or Stuffed Animal

DIRECTIONS:

1. Please pick a story from a previous Lesson. (You may also pick a book from your home or library that your child is able to read.)

2. Explain to your child that pets and/or stuffed animals love to hear stories. It makes them feel so loved.

3. If you have a pet, allow your child to read the story to your pet.

4. If you do not have a pet, ask your child to pick his favorite stuffed animal and read it the story.

5. This is a fun activity to allow your child to do each day.

● ● ●

Activity 12

MATERIALS:

- ☐ Stories From Previous Lessons

DIRECTIONS:

1. Now that your child has become more fluent in his reading, pointing to words as he reads might be slowing his reading down. Allow him to try reading without pointing to words.

2. Please select a story from a previous Lesson. (You may also choose a book from your home or library that your child is able to read.)

3. Ask your child to read a story to you without pointing.

4. If you see that your child is getting lost in his reading by not pointing to the words, please try to use the guided reading strips or place a piece of paper under the line of text he is reading before going back to pointing to each individual word.

I like cats

Who are you

This is fun

| . | ! | ? |

Jack

Jack likes

Jack likes to

Jack likes to swim

Jack likes to swim in

Jack likes to swim in the

Jack likes to swim in the lake.

Read the text 3 times. Place your finger on each star as you read the words.

Lesson 38

Where does Jack like to swim?	Draw a picture of Jack swimming in the lake.
_____	
Read and trace the word:	
likes	

The muffin is in the basket.

The muffin is in the basket.

 The muffin is in the basket.

The girl pets a gray dolphin.

The girl pets a gray dolphin.

The girl pets a gray dolphin.

cut along line

The duck flew over the large boat.

The duck flew over the large boat.

 The duck flew over the large boat.

We will eat peas and carrots for dinner.

We will eat peas and carrots for dinner.

 We will eat peas and carrots for dinner.

Lesson 38

Fluency Self Check

What does my reading sound like?

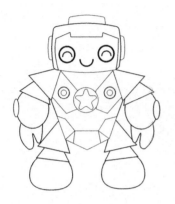  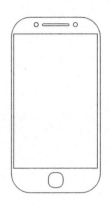

I read with expression.

I phrased the words together.

<u>Our Beach Trip</u>

I love to go to the beach with my mom, dad, brother, and sister! I like when my dad helps me make a sand castle. We use my bucket and shovel to make the castle big. We look for seashells to put on the castle.

My mom packs a yummy lunch to take to the beach. We sit in the sand and eat our lunch. The birds like to eat our crumbs.

My brother, sister, and I like to jump in the waves after lunch. We see who can jump the highest. We like to look for small fish in the waves too. When we see a fish, we try to catch it.

Beach days are so fun!

121 Words